Finding Love *and* Healing
in the pen!

Turning the Pages Toward My Destiny

by Kimberly T. Mitchell

His Unlikely Source

FINDING LOVE *and* HEALING
in the pen!

by Kimberly T. Mitchell

published by:
Books by HHC
Yonkers, NY 10704

This book is an autobiographical testimony. Names were altered to maintain the anonymity of the characters in the story.

No parts of this book may be reproduced, stored in a retrieval system, or transmitted by any means without the written permission of the author.

AUTHOR:	KIMBERLY T. MITCHELL
COVER DESIGN | TYPESET:	DEESIGNZ WEB & GRAPHICS STUDIO
INTERPRETIVE EDITORIAL & REWRITE:	DENEEN G. MATTHEWS
CATEGORIES:	FAITH & INSPIRATION, NON-FICTION, AUTOBIOGRAPHY
ISBN:	978-0-692-14185-4

PRINTED IN THE UNITED STATES OF AMERICA
PAPERBACK, 136 PAGES

© 2018 FINDING LOVE & HEALING IN THE PEN . KIMBERLY T. MITCHELL ALL RIGHTS RESERVED.

Finding Love and Healing in the Pen!
Healing Deep Within

Healing begins within;
Before the words are spoken;
Formed from a place of vulnerability;
A place of honesty and openness.
Deep within —
The place known only to you and God,
Tis true,
That He loves you and hasn't forgotten.
Then He sends His messengers,
To call to you and draw you out
From the deep,
Chaotic place into a place of purpose
Through words that carry light and life.
Through the pen
And with love,
The healing process then unfolds…

FEAR WILL DO ONE THING
— HOLD YOU BACK!

DEDICATION
FINDING LOVE AND HEALING IN THE PEN!

Finding Love and Healing in the Pen is dedicated to:

- Those who haven't given up on me.
- Those who stood by me while I learned to stand on my own and walk with confidence.
- My parents, Hattie and Victor Mitchell.
- My children, Alexis and Mark Mitchell; thank you, Lord, for trusting me with your precious gifts.
- My brother, Jamal Mitchell.
- My mentors:

  Rev. Dr. Jeffery R. Wheeler
  MOUNT CALVARY CME *"THE PROMISE"* CHURCH

  Rev. Dr. Regina Reese-Young
  ST. JOHN CME CHURCH

- Thank you Hope and Deneen for taking me in.

I thank God for each one of you every day!

Numbers 6:24-26 *"May the Lord bless you and protect you. May the Lord smile on you and be gracious to you. May the Lord show you his favor and give you his peace."* (NLT)

FINDING LOVE AND HEALING IN THE PEN!
TABLE OF CONTENTS

Introduction ix

CHAPTER 1: The Setting 1

CHAPTER 2: Fitting In 12

CHAPTER 3: When the Pen Stopped 16

CHAPTER 4: Desperate 70

CHAPTER 5: Release the Hostages! 77

CHAPTER 6: Unfinished Business 80

CHAPTER 7: Baptism Sunday 85

CHAPTER 8: Pieces of the Puzzle 88

CHAPTER 9: Excuse Me While I Change 94

CHAPTER 10: What Will Your Legacy Be? 98

CHAPTER 11: New Journey 102

CHAPTER 12: Being Validated 106

CHAPTER 13: Led by God, Lead by Example 109

CHAPTER 14: Who Will You Be Loyal To? 114

Introduction
Finding Love and Healing in the Pen!

That particular morning, I found myself jotting down every word from that Sunday morning sermon – every word and every utterance – even down to the description of the atmosphere in the sanctuary. It was then that I felt a *"new"* begin to stir within – a new beginning, a new start, and a new desire to find out more about this faith in God, who claimed to possess unlimited love for me. What became utterly clear at that very moment was what I was doing to myself wasn't working.

Week after week, I became more devoted; and my soul, an empty reservoir, searched for the water that would fill every dry place. Still broken, yet the more I listened, the more diligent I became. I hurried home to write down and further explore the nuggets I received. It was as if my hands were cupped together carefully in order to preserve what I was given. I was intent not to lose any of it and afraid what I had obtained would be gone before I was able to capture it all. Each passing week, I became stronger and continued to run until I no longer felt the urge to stop at the store just across the bridge to purchase my next bottle that I once thought contained the antidote to life's woes.

The inventory that rested on the shelves of that establishment had power to ruin many lives. Oh, but be ever so careful lest you fall prey and become victim to its tight grip and your mind reprogrammed to depend upon what was kept behind those doors. It will offer no resolve to your life issues but only create new ones fully loaded with consequences excluded from the warning label.

I became more and more tenacious in my seeking until what began as my running pass the store became an ability to walk. No longer did I respond to the imaginary voice of the bottled contents that used to call my name; no longer did I need to drown my sorrows in rum and vodka to ease the hurt and pain. Those temporary fixes were inadequate to deliver me or provide the permanent healing I so longed for. It was true, He loved me; God always loved me, and my eyes were opening, and then, it was there – that's when... *I saw Him.*

He was right beside me, alongside me, composing and orchestrating the mess I made of my life. He was molding and handcrafting me into His wonderful masterpiece. The good news is that He's waiting to do the same for you.

During my journey, when I began to recognize His nudgings, I grew fascinated with the characters of the bible and the stories they told through their lives. Their testimonies spoke of wisdom, faith, and strength. Their lives became unrecognizable as they held on and trusted in God even when man overlooked them. It was then that I realized how we are very similar to the bible characters and how we share so much through common obstacles and experiences. There are even times when we feel overlooked by God while in search of our purpose. Oftentimes, He only releases just enough wisdom for each particular season. The biographical accounts in the bible bring light and revelation that help guide us on our journey. Lessons told through the lives of His unlikely sources inspire, motivate, and help us navigate through the challenges that arise in our lives.

You, too, are a unique story and a key to unlock someone else's personal prison. I am a firm believer that we all have a story to be told and we share that testimony with others through our gifts (writing, speaking, singing, preaching, teaching, and much more).

As I continue to submit to God's will, He's teaching me how to wait upon Him and endure. It's important to remain aware of His presence and recognize the clues left along the path that will ultimately lead to who and what we are destined to become. A transformation must take place, and the seed within us must be properly nourished and cultivated.

Throughout different seasons, God provides tools to help us advance through each level. These tools strengthen us during the valley seasons and equip us to climb each level of our mountain experiences.

THE NEW JOURNEY

Why are we so easily impacted by what is contrary rather than what is agreeable? Why we are more receptive to settle for less than our true value?

The twists and turns are inevitable; however, we must persevere. There is greater waiting at the end. Vigilance is needed to combat discouragement and despair; careful not be distracted by how bad things appear. For some reason, we often think the record of our past mistakes has rendered us unworthy to receive anything good from God.

We really need to monitor how much time we spend around negative influences. We do a good enough job of bearing down on ourselves by way of our own thoughts. The words we think and words we speak about our lives will either water the seeds or feed the weeds. The greatest challenge is learning to quiet our inner voice and move beyond our own negative self-talk. We create so many scenarios in our minds about situations before they even have a chance to play out without considering that every storm has a proper place in our lives and carries what is needed to move us into subsequent phases.

We are already delivered, yet we must endure the process. Deliverance can come in different ways – some by flood and others by fire. God can choose to remove us from the flood or fire or wash us with the floodwaters and/or purify us through the flames. Ultimately, we grow as a result of the trials and tests and gain newfound strength as a result.

Oftentimes, the individual pieces may not paint a clear picture, but if we keep exercising faith and journal our experiences, we will begin to see what was being portrayed in the obscurity. Placing the puzzle pieces in their assigned places will unveil the picture and reveal the purpose hidden amidst the scattered parts. Suddenly, we discover just how far we've traveled, just how much we've advanced, and the accomplishments we've secured on this new journey.

There is something absolutely incredible about a notepad and pen. God holds the pen – the instrument, which is us. I relate our messes to the ink that the pen dispenses, which, at first, has not yet formed anything recognizable. However, if we allow the hands of our Father to guide the pen strokes, something beautiful and unique will emerge. He will pen the perfect story, and the main theme will bring light and hope to others who live in darkness and despair. Ultimately, a wonderfully handwritten, one-of-a-kind masterpiece is rendered.

Be careful to take notice of how His love graces each page. We don't want to dismiss that He has always been there, and He is the author of our story.

2 Corinthians 3:2 *"You yourselves are our letter, written on our hearts, known and read by everyone."* (NCV)

UNLIKELY SOURCES

Unlikely is defined as not likely, improbable, an unlikely outcome, likely to fail, unpromising.

Source is defined as a cause or starting point, someone or something that provides what is needed.

(Source: Merriam Webster Online Dictionary)

A source can also refer to a person used to bring life to a hopeless situation through the message they carry on behalf of our heavenly Father – our Creator.

The characters in the bible had a great deal in common. Those men, women, and children were often among the outcasts and undesirables. Many went on and became faithful and devoted stewards over the assignments God placed on their lives. Although they made mistakes, many were restored by the power of repentance and the mercy of a loving and just God. After they turned away from their wrong doing, quite often they displayed an even greater zeal for God and testified before others of His love, faithfulness, grace, and mercy. Their inward transformations sparked interesting dialogue among onlookers who noticed the outward evidence of change through their deportment and the marvels God performed through them. They also left behind recorded accounts of their trials and triumphs for our edification.

As a result, I gleaned wisdom concerning my own personal challenges and realized how much God desired a heart-to-heart, one-on-one, intimate relationship with me. The setbacks were divinely orchestrated so that He would be glorified in my life. What I experienced in my past failed in comparison to what God had in store for my future.

I am one of His chosen vessels – one of His unlikely sources.

CHAPTER ONE

THE SETTING

What started as a seemingly perfect beginning somehow slowly turned into a fast-paced drama full of secrets and events that should have concluded in tragedy. Instead, these scenarios evolved into a beautifully written love story between the Father and me, His prodigal daughter.

The difference between how my life began and where it headed appeared as though I tripped and fell into someone else's story and left the comfort of my own behind. In fact, that's exactly what occurred. I almost literally became an entirely different person.

***

Growing up, our house seemed to be the biggest on the block. When you turned onto our street, quite noticeably, 426 stood out from the others and was situated midway the block. The house was adorned with white aluminum siding and the front face embellished with pink-and-yellow colored bricks. Our sun porch boasted large, beautiful windows decorated with flowers.

The hedges out front stood at least 6-feet tall, like a green fence that guarded the most beautiful rose bush and flower garden directly beyond it and extended along the side. My dad always used the tallest ladder he owned to climb to the top and keep the hedges neatly manicured.

The smooth paved walkway led up to the seven steps to the front door, and a small light sat perfectly above the heavy doors, illuminating the way at night for both occupants and visitors alike.

These were the most recent renovations to 426 – the second round in fact – a much better representation than the former red porch with yellow posts, but I did miss the wall on the side of the steps that permitted me to swing back and forth as I sat. The yard around back was plush with fresh-cut grass and a plum tree, and another small garden complimented the well-cared-for landscape. My father had a knack for transitioning the old into what emerged as new and beautiful.

426 housed many memories filled with both hope and despair; treasured and precious memories that transcended beyond what was happening at any given time – never absent of the sense of security beyond its walls that guarded against the notion that all was ever lost. Through the many renditions of change, there was one thing that remained – the love that was established between my family and me and the bond I had with my older brother. No matter what I faced in the world outside of 426, I was always able to return, to come back home. I never strayed beyond the boundary of the love of my family. Everything I endured contributed to the woman I am today, and the invisible scars paid it forward for the strength I obtained along the way.

Every Sunday and during holidays, our street was filled with parked cars, some double-parked and others blocking entrances to driveways. When the time came for family and visitors to leave and return to their own residences, normalcy resumed accompanied by quietness, followed by what often felt like emptiness. Our house, however, even on regular days, was occupied with family from the attic to the basement. This was my normal, and sanctuary was only found in my bedroom or the bathroom when added privacy was warranted.

Champ and Spike, the household pets, occupied the basement; that's where they retired at night to sleep. The two never really got along, so separate living quarters were in order with tightly secured doors between the two of them.

The second and third floors were where my grandparents, aunts, and uncle lived. Spike, an unusual black dog, belonged to them. He looked like a cocker spaniel and had a bad attitude. He never moved out of your way when you came upstairs for a visit. In fact, he stared you down and emitted a low growl under his breath, as if to ask if you were sure you wanted to venture his way.

I lived on the first floor with my parents, my older brother, and our dog, Champ, a beautiful black-and-white German shepherd. Duke, a handsomely tanned German shepherd, came to live with us after Champ was kidnapped. At least, that was my assumption. There was no other explanation why he didn't return home where he was treated so well. We missed Champ after he was gone. He had a more serious temperament and was very protective of his family. Although we didn't develop very much of a bond, Champ still left a void in us all, and I was left with personal feelings of hurt that I kept to myself.

When we had company, Champ loved to play tag with the kids. Sometimes he chased us into the bathtub after we taunted him with the chant, *"Here comes Champion."* The tub was actually home base, and after all the kids jumped in, he turned and ran out of the bathroom. I'm still not sure what that meant. Champ probably just wanted to chase us annoying kids away.

Though Champ loved to play, he also had a bit of a bite. He wasn't like Duke, who was like one of the kids. I'm sure if Duke had lived longer, he would have developed his bite as well, but Duke left us. One day, he was playing at the park and attempted to jump over a rail. He didn't jump quite high enough to clear the rail and broke his leg, and the doctors couldn't fix it. I really don't think they knew how. I never accepted that Duke had died. As far as I was concerned, they put him to sleep, and that was exactly how I left it – Duke was asleep.

Shutting out unpleasant things became a quickly developed behavior but also became increasingly difficult to manage. Resentment from unresolved hurt and pain settled in, and if anyone tried to intrude upon the place where I stored and guarded my unpleasant things, I reacted defensively and became easily offended. This was just the beginning, however, of a quiet but vicious storm that grew stronger and became more destructive. I wasn't equipped to deal with my feelings or express myself when things became uncomfortable. Pretending that things remained the same as I remembered them altered my reality. I was not aware that I was in the preliminary stages of compromising my own happiness and freedom. I had not yet started to look for things to help me ease the pain of life's disappointments.

I held tightly to the pleasant memories of living at home – at 426 – complete with the smell of fresh-baked pies and cakes and huge meals shared with both families. When my mother and grandmother cooked, they always shared what they prepared, and dinner often turned into a family gathering occasion.

Inside our home, the walls were painted white and decorated with pictures. The kitchen was the exception, however, covered with orange-and-white wallpaper with tiny pictures of fruit. The chairs at the kitchen table, where we sat as a family to eat breakfast and dinner, were the coolest. I spent a lot of time sitting at the table, eating, drawing, doing homework, or just spinning in the chairs. The backs of the chairs were brown, and you could see through them. I often sat and spun around while my mom busied herself with cooking, baking, cleaning, or talking on the phone.

My bedroom was right off the kitchen and was adjacent to another room in the house. The room had what I loved to call a super-secret wall, which was not uncommon for a child less than ten years old. This secret wall served as an alternate doorway to my parents' room, without me getting up and walking to the door. It was an easy out in case the bumps in the night became unbearable. All I had to do was crack open the secret wall and call for help. Almost every room in the house had a second doorway that led into a different room or out in the hallway. It was a pretty cool setup.

My parents were great at providing all I needed and things I never thought I would. I was brought up with a strong foundation built on love – the kind spoken of in the bible – the God unconditional kind of love. So how did I deviate so far from my upbringing and why? Although the answer not a simple one, I ascertained that even I had to go through many different transformations, just like my family home at 426.

426 underwent several transformations over the years. My father was very gifted in the do-it-yourself projects area. The building changed on the inside as well as on the outside. He added rooms to keep up with the needs of a growing family. After my grandparents moved out, the door between the second and third floors was removed, and it became one huge apartment. My parents were on the second floor, and my brother and I took the upstairs third-floor attic, which became two bedrooms, a living room, and a bathroom. Later, the first-floor downstairs was renovated and rented out.

***

Similarly, the same takes place with each of us. We undergo inward and outward transformations accompanied by seasons of discomfort, but, in the end, what was old will be made new under the construction and blueprint plans of our heavenly Father. It all begins with our relationship with Him.

***

My parents' union was a great close-up example of partnership – oneness joined by God. They were both great providers and both shared in the financial responsibility for the family. My father was employed with the Unites States Postal Service, a well-rounded engineer by trade, and a carpenter in his spare time, who made sure things in our home were in working order. My mother, outside of her nine-to-five office job as an office manager, kept our home comfortable and peaceful. She prepared our meals, fuel for our physical bodies, and made sure we attended church where we were fed spiritually, and the principals of trustworthiness and faithfulness were taught to us early on.

By the time I was in fifth grade, I was trusted to walk home by myself. After I arrived, I sat at the table in the fun chair and took the phone with its mile-long cord from the wall and called my mom at work. The receptionist already knew who was on the line. She always answered, *"Kim, is that you? How are you, Darling? Hold on, let me put you right through to your mom."*

After I spoke with my mother, I placed the phone back on the receiver, pulled out my books from my bag, and placed them on the table. I wasn't at home alone for very long, only for about ten minutes as a matter of fact. The first car that pulled into the driveway was my dad's. I heard the door open and close, and at exactly 3:30, he came in through the back door. An hour later, like clockwork, the second car pulled into the driveway. By that time, my homework was usually done, and I was in my room. I peeked out from my bedroom window, and there was my mother.

My parents laid a solid foundation, and they provided my first lessons in faith. As a result, I learned to believe things were actually going to happen even before it was obvious that they would. It's like the example of my parents coming home daily. I never had to look out of the window, but I knew they would arrive. I didn't know much about faith on my own, but even my ability to rely on my parents taught me the elementary lessons of faith that relate to developing and building confidence in people.

***

On Saturday mornings, I either heard the chatter of my parents speaking to each other or my mom talking on the phone. Sometimes, I heard my dad's voice outside speaking with the neighbors while they did their chores out in the yard – trimming hedges, cutting grass, and washing the cars – weather permitting. Their hand-washed and waxed vehicles lined along the sides of the houses shined so brightly they could have very easily been mistaken for new models driven off the showroom floor.

More often, the scent of fresh homemade biscuits along with the aroma of coffee, bacon, eggs, and grits from the kitchen filled the air and stirred me from my sleep. Occasionally, I was awakened to pancakes with the coveted sweet syrup, and on more rare occasions, cereal made the weekend menu, but neither was very filling or nutritious. I reckon they were the occasional treats reserved for every once in a while, but the challenge was that often I didn't survive hunger till lunchtime. As a result, my mother was often confronted with the complaining groans and whining of a hungry child well before the next scheduled meal.

McDonald's was another once-in-a-lifetime treat; especially since my parents were determined to completely steer clear of that establishment. Come on, you remember the excitement as a child when you were permitted to stand in line and order a happy meal, don't you? *"Eating out"* was a treat even amongst my friends on the block. We were super excited when we were able to score a pizza, and even then, our parents were reluctant. Ironically then, home-cooked meals were not as rare and infrequent as they are now.

I was raised during an era when everyone on the block knew who you were and knew your family. People back then were very courteous and neighborly toward one another even while they busied themselves and went about their regularly scheduled chores and errands.

My mom shopped at four different grocery stores and three department stores and came home with the car loaded with all sorts of goodies. Sometimes, between mom's choir practice and our household chores, we visited a member from church, Mrs. Althea Mae Davis, but I didn't mind. In addition to the stores we frequented, a visit to her home was indeed quite pleasurable for a young child. Mrs. Davis made the most outstanding seven-layer cakes for us to take home, and she always fixed me a nice serving of Jell-O and whipped cream while we sat and visited. My mom tried to put up a fuss, but Mrs. Davis won every time. It was as if God blessed me with a third grandmother, and I had no objections.

In order to tag along on those shopping outings and visits, I had to catch my mom before she left the house to run her errands. I think she tried to sneak out because parents, especially moms, knew that if they took the children along, they'd spend more money than they planned. I, on the other hand, always got sleepy from riding around and rarely got anything extra, especially if I complained. I didn't mind much, because my mom always bought me the prettiest dresses in any and every color as long as it passed the twirl test. Most times, dresses were reserved for church and special occasions. When I was all dressed up, I felt like the belle of the ball. I spun around, and the hem of my dress twirled, as if air had filled the hem and it took on a life of its own. I wore the matching lace-trimmed socks and fancy patent leather shoes that made noise on the tile or wooden floors when I walked. I often tried to emulate my mother who walked so gracefully. Bottom line was if I missed a shopping outing, the disappointment passed quickly when my mother brought home surprise packages and things unexpected.

I had plenty of toys, books, and games inside to keep me occupied at home. One of my favorite past times, when the weather allowed, was to swing on the beautiful green-and-white swing set in the backyard. Because it was only used on weekends when school was out or chores were completed, the swing set was in like-new condition.

Some of the neighborhood kids who came over to play loved the swing set too. They stretched their legs out as far as they could and pretended to reach the top of the tree. Many would swing as high as they could and then let go and jump off the swings. The thrill and risky activity of momentary suspension in mid-air and then landing safely seemed to excite them, but it wasn't for me. That was just not a risk I was willing to take. I preferred an enjoyable swing and found safety in what I could see in my immediate perimeter.

***

Looking back, as a child growing in faith, I saw how fear could become a hindrance. It surely had the potential to keep you from moving forward and taking the necessary risks, or better yet, leaps of faith – the act of letting go and letting God, as they say. The seed within begins to call out and encourages us to hurdle toward our destiny. I realized that when we do what we are asked by our heavenly Father, he always provides what is needed. Remember, He can see the entire and complete picture and would never ask anything of us that He hasn't already supplied the necessary tools and resources needed to honor His request.

***

You see, my parents not only worked very hard to provide for our needs – food, shelter, clothing, and our basic life necessities –during the summer or extended school closings, we took long getaways, vacationed at our other home in Ocean City, Maryland, or visited with family in North Carolina, South Carolina, Florida, Washington, or Canada. They provided those opportunities to show us just how much more was available to us. When we were obedient, we were rewarded with treats and special trips like Disney World or other amusement theme parks.

Growing up, there wasn't a season I didn't enjoy. There was always something happening and something to plan for. Christmas was my absolute favorite holiday. There was something very special about sitting in the living room, eating a candy cane, sipping on hot chocolate, listening to *Silent Night*, and looking at the angel on top of the tree while the beautiful lights danced off the wall and shone all around me. The tree always seemed small in comparison to the number of gifts underneath. There was always an overflow; as if my parents had the stores redirect their shipments of toys, clothes, and electronics to our home. I always knew who *"Santa"* was in my home, but it was still fun to watch the holiday movies and programs.

My brother and I were kept occupied while my parents prepared for the holiday. When I became antsy, my mom locked herself in the bedroom, and the basement became my dad's workshop for gifts like my Barbie Dream Home that just so happened to appear fully assembled on Christmas morning on the table in the middle of the floor. This continued down to the grandchildren – trains, Power Wheels cars, and motorcycles arranged in the middle of the living room and dining room floors.

My surroundings were always filled with joyful experiences, so anything that disrupted that flow was difficult to deal with. As a result, when I encountered loss, especially of a pet or a close loved one, I shut it out. For quite a while, I thought it was going well and that I was getting along and navigating well through life.

Whenever I had to attend a funeral, I kept my head down and never focused on the coffin in front of me. In my mind, I sent my loved one on a trip somewhere enjoyable, but never accepted that death was the culprit, and there was definitely no thought taken for them being buried underground. I created fantasies of happiness to counteract feelings of discomfort, hoping one day they would be authenticated, which was much easier to address than the current reality.

I refused to accept that their absence was final, and, as a child, that became my coping mechanism. I needed to have that final mental vision of my loved one alive and well, not laid out in a display box we call a coffin. During funeral services, I spent the two hours or so focused on everything else except the body in the box in the front of the room. Even when the family got up for the processional and the casket viewing, I faced the opposite direction rather than to look on and face the fact that I would never see them again and deal with the pain involved with acceptance and the dread of missing them. This became a habit I formed with great perfection. I learned early on how to deal with something painful by not dealing with it at all, even the death of our pet, Duke. Nothing whatsoever was going to compromise my happy place. I learned to cover the pain involved with loss or just pretend it never existed.

CHAPTER TWO
FITTING IN

I have always seemed to do things a bit differently from others. My approach to dealing with loss, grief, and pain remained an ongoing issue and began to escalate. While I tried diligently to contain one area of my life and maintain anonymity and *"normalcy,"* the other areas of my life refused to allow me to fly under the radar and remain undetected. I trusted and depended on the life I knew before life interrupted it, and all I wanted was what was to remain undisturbed.

Essentially, the truth is that I am different; we are all different and unique and not designed to fit in or be *"normal."* Many of our outward physical factors can be covered or altered. For instance, I was born left-handed but re-trained at a young age to reach with and write with my right hand.

***

What sets us apart is often displayed early in life, then concealed until the appointed time. Our innate gifts, those we are endowed with at birth, go into hibernation where they are protected until we mature and are disciplined to guard and steward well over them.

***

Most often when babies learn to walk, the first stage, crawling, is often motivated by their ambition to lay hold of something spotted across the room. A small child will crawl and/or pull themselves up with the aid of a table or other object in the path of their conquest. I was told that I rolled, as if my legs would not cooperate and carry me where I wanted to go as quickly as I desired. I found an alternate method of accomplishing the same task, even if it wasn't the most conventional.

I also had some learning challenges during my grade school years. Overall, my grades weren't the best, but I loved to read and write and received outstanding grades in spelling. I learned to persevere through the challenges and difficulties while seizing opportunities to disprove opinions contrary to my success by exploiting my strengths.

***

What appeared then as setbacks now seem like divine set-ups. Quite honestly, I can attest that every misstep was the right step ordered and even ordained by God, and nothing is a surprise to Him. Before we were formed in our mothers' wombs, He knew us. I'm convinced that we operated in our gifts even as we learned to walk and talk. If we had the ability to discern, we may have tuned in and caught a quick glimpse of them early on before they were sealed and secured until the proper season.

Most of us enjoy the budding of spring flowers and the fragrant aroma emitted from the petals but readily ignore that the seed in the ground had to die in order to put forth new life.

Consider a seed planted in a garden – in the heart of the earth – hidden from human observation. Watering and ploughing the ground is an integral part of the development process. Although the package may display a beautiful snapshot of what was planted, early onset does not yet reveal the end result. Seedtime and harvest must be fully executed before the results of that seed become apparent. Seed is associated with the act of planting. Time entails the watering, cultivation, and waiting. This is generally the longest part of the process until harvest, which presents us with the burden of proof of what was planted.

While our seed is covered in a deep place, oftentimes a dark place, it undergoes stages of changes and is ultimately transformed. This illustration parallels our transformation process. Just as the seed planted in the ground must die in order to undergo transformation, so must we in order to put off the former and become full grown, mature, and amply prepared to serve according to our purpose.

On the part of the observer, the process often reveals what may seem inconsistent with the intended results. Much of the work is done within, hidden and without observation. Onlookers may be tempted to draw conclusions based on our seasons of trials, tests, failures, and triumphs that may obscure the intended outcome. Trials and tests are preparatory tools that teach us how to survive the dying process so that we may sustain during harvest season and cover new ground up ahead.

We are not provided the exact time that our seed will put forth fruit in the manner God originally intended, but what is certain is that we will reap a favorable harvest in due time if we trust God and remain obedient to His will.

Bear in mind that spring will eventually arrive; the old will pass away, and all things will be made new.

Stay in the process, stay focused, and don't get sidetracked and lost in feelings of hopelessness. He promised to make all things beautiful in time.

***

It is imperative to hear and discern the voice of God while eliminating distractions. He will make our enemies our footstool and cause us to overcome and taste victory. Neither the purpose nor the message is solely about us. We are all vessels and instruments to be used for His service to testify to others who need to be encouraged in their faith. We each become a unique message sent to display, minister God's love, and let our light shine that He may be glorified through us.

God's *unlikely sources* aren't designed to fit in but to be consecrated for His service and set apart for His glory. When that became clearer to me, everything else became lessons I knew I was designated to learn.

CHAPTER THREE
WHEN THE PEN STOPPED

Proverbs 4:23 *"Keep your heart with all diligence, for out of it spring the issues of life."* (NKJV)

I had no problem expressing myself. Writing letters was my means of escape – my place of solitude and retreat. Whatever I couldn't verbalize, I wrote about. It wasn't until I was without pen and pad that I was made aware of its importance.

I longed for what I loved, but I wasn't quite sure why I stopped writing. I missed the letters I penned when I was younger and, oh, not to mention, my pink-and-red diary where I sorted out all my thoughts and feelings – the good ones, the bad ones, and the not-to-mention ones... I started keeping record of the wrong things and left my heart unprotected and opened to assault.

***

When I was old enough to cross the street on my own, I made frequent trips to the local stationery store or the greeting card section of CVS to select birthday, anniversary, or just-thinking-of-you cards. I spent hours upon hours reading each card until I found the one that best spoke from my heart and most adequately described my relationship with the person for whom the card was intended.

On so many occasions, I was confronted with the question my mother asked most predictably, *"Kimberly, where have you been all this time?"* A simple exercise for others was a very intricate occurrence that held great importance for me. I couldn't just grab any card from the display; the words had to be just right. I also enjoyed writing notes, letters, and poems to my parents or to whomever I wanted to share what was in my heart. Truthfully, what I received in return was the much-needed attention I sought as a result of how others responded to those gestures. I almost literally wore my heart on my sleeve without the smallest notion that it needed protecting. It wasn't long before that part of me was lost and never to be recovered, so I thought. I went from giving away freely what was in my heart to locking it away and barricading it behind the boundaries roped off with yellow tape marked, *Caution!*

My First Love

Teenage love... something we've all experienced, right? You know, that first love that is supposed to last longer than eternity – where the break up was so tragic that you felt like you were dying? "And the Oscar goes to..." WRONG! We barely knew how to love ourselves, much less another person.

Once again, a familiar concept emerged – parents knew best – and were one hundred and ten percent committed to protecting us. As teenagers, we were not mature enough to pursue the places that an untamed heart would lead us.

Adults have argued and proven that love at thirteen (puppy love as some call it) doesn't really exist. In fact, if we fail to acknowledge the context of 1 Corinthians, chapter thirteen, that outlines the characteristics of love and the degree of love displayed by Christ's sacrifice for us, even at age 113, we would fail to know the true meaning of love. Yes, that may be a bit of a stretch yet entirely true. Admittedly, it took quite some time for me to gain understanding of the meaning and intent of true and divine love.

***

I was thirteen years old, and I thought I apprehended it – love, of course – the kind that never ends. David and I had so much in common, and we were in love. He was the first guy I met who shared my love for writing. This was perfect because I lived in New

York and he lived in Virginia, and the nine-hour distance between us almost seemed non-existent. Even more ideal was the fact that our parents knew each other, and we had family in Virginia we visited occasionally. Besides, nothing or no one was going to keep us apart.

Outside of our family visits to Virginia, we spent endless hours talking on the phone. I got in huge trouble because clearly, at age thirteen, I was not responsible for paying the phone bill and had no idea of the cost associated with our long-distance chats.

One day, my parents received an enormous phone bill in the mail, and, oh my goodness, I just knew I would be grounded forever when I heard them discussing how the house budget was affected because of all the long-distance phone calls. This was also when I learned that I wasn't a very good liar.

My father summoned me into the room and asked sternly, *"Kimberly, who made all of these phone calls?"*

I sort of did this shoulder shrug thing and responded awkwardly, *"I don't know,"* which only provoked him to dial the number that was displayed repeatedly on the bill. I prayed under my breath that David wouldn't answer, but to my detriment, he did; and my father asked, *"Young man, what is your name?"*

How embarrassing! I cringed as I thought of what else he would say. Needless to report, I was grounded before he returned the receiver to the base. *In case anyone is confused, before cordless phones and cell phones, we had house phones with a base, receiver, and cord plugged into a power source in the wall.*

At thirteen years of age, I was not even allowed to be in a relationship. My parents insisted that my efforts be directed toward education and self-discovery. Apparently, they were all too well acquainted with the distractions involved in focusing so much of my time and attention on someone else at such a young age.

After the phone bill fiasco, our phone calls were limited to a half-hour, with permission, of course. However, when David and I weren't on the phone, we wrote letters. We received letters from each other at least every other week. As soon as I received a letter in the mail, I hurried to my room to read what he had written and quickly drafted my response. My goal was to get a return letter sent off at least by the very next day. Fortunately, there was a mailbox right at the top of the block, so I didn't have to ask my parents to mail them, but make no mistake, they were fully aware of our correspondence.

Wow! Did we *really* have that much to say to each other? We did, apparently, because this routine continued for three consecutive years. We began each letter with the title of a song in the subject line. One of our favorite songs was "Make It Last Forever," by Keith Sweat. I'm not sure how appropriate of a selection that was for young teens, and just what *did* we know about forever? Could we realistically continue that long without interruption?

We poured out our hearts filled with longing for the next time we would see each other and exchanged so many I-miss-you sentiments that filled up the miles between us. We also never missed sending birthday cards, holiday cards, or just-because-you-are-on-my-mind cards. This was ideal for the girl who still believed in fairy tales — perhaps it was the words on paper that spoke to the ideal in my heart. Quite naively, I thought anyone who articulated from that special place had to be true blue.

David invited me into a place that felt safe. He knew there were unresolved thoughts and feelings I kept secret and urged me to talk them through. He somehow became the calm in the midst of the storm that was raging inside of me. Somehow, he touched the girl I was before life interrupted. Later, I realized that the writing was less about who was on the other side of my letters and more about who I was writing for – me – and the dependency upon the word exchange that created a place where I retreated for safety. This too was short-lived when reality crept in.

I was headed straight for a place my young, teenage mind was not prepared for. I thought everything would remain as perfect and pristine as the fairytale princess love stories I read about or the teenage hit pop songs from the '80s we listened to and sang along. The ideal young romance, when all was pure and innocent, and the line was drawn at holding hands and maybe a little bit of kissing, was what I fantasized about.

Well, life inserted itself again, and the ideal I created as my security blanket now became vulnerable to attack. I learned that David had another friend who was more advanced than I was and willing to go where I would not. Her name was Angela, and she was the poster child for fast girls. I called her "Fast Tail Angela," and she played a part in David and my breakup.

One evening during the school week, my cousin called. She caught me by surprise because she hardly ever called. We exchanged greetings; then she asked if David and I were still seeing each other.

"Yes, we are," I responded cautiously.

There was a long pause followed by dead silence. Then she spoke.

First my heart sank, and then I went numb as she told me about Angela and that she and David were a hot item. Angela was one of those girls willing to go all the way and give away what was meant to remain chaste. David and I had previous discussions about this very topic, and he assured me that he was fine with the fact that I wasn't ready. Little did I know, he was fine getting it from someone else.

I was devastated by the news. I felt betrayed and wanted him to experience the pain I felt. Holding back tears, I ended the call quite abruptly. As soon as the phone returned to the base, I grabbed a bunch of cards and letters he sent and scribbled LIES in large bold letters across his words on the paper and mailed them back.

A week later, his cousin called in an attempt to intercede on his behalf and explained how hurt David was when he received the letters. David grabbed the receiver from his cousin and began to speak.

"Kim, I ..."

Before he finished his sentence, I confronted him.

He lied.

I cried.

I thought I could never forgive him for what he had done. His betrayal made forgiveness extremely difficult for me. David was my safe place, though I'm sure he was unaware of how much I depended on him.

Life landed another devastating blow, and I had no outlet to express my feelings and no one I could trust them to. Besides, my relationship with David was what I wrote about and now that was nonexistent. I didn't know what to do. It hurt, and I recognized the vaguely familiar pain of loss I experience when Duke died, but this was different. David was still alive and so was I, but *we* were not a reality any longer. I didn't wear my heart on my sleeve, but it was wrapped around the words notated on paper. I stopped writing at a time when it was probably most crucial.

***

Nevertheless, here we are presented with a perfect opportunity to admit and acknowledge that our parents really do know what's best. They understand the need for maturity and discipline and how not to be carried away by our raw emotions. They are equipped with wisdom to help us remain watchful along this life journey. Potholes are inevitable, but, oftentimes, there are warning signs alerting us to danger up ahead. Much like today's smartphones and technological devices, parents have built-in settings that send notifications and alerts before we malfunction. Signals and warnings, such as "slow" and "slippery up ahead," instruct us and call our attention to take safety precautions.

The same is also extended to other adults who invest in our well-being. Because we are young and lack life experience, we are prone to believe that they are overreacting, and we disregard the GPS in them along with the directions given to us.

Well, I, for one, ignored the warnings and indicators that could have kept me from quite a few head-on collisions. Once we open the door to deceit and retaliate with cover-ups for wrongdoing, we eventually arrive at a destination called disobedience.

***

As I progressed through my teenage years, I kept a lot of my thoughts and feelings hidden. I really needed to find a way to escape my feelings and did my best to keep it together. I didn't want to feel what I was feeling. Seemingly, everyone else moved on almost effortlessly when leaving old loves behind. I too wanted to apprehend whatever made it so easy for others to abort, disregard, and pass go, but my conscience would not agree.

One of my favorite places to retreat when I was upset was the roof outside my bedroom window. Often, I sat quietly looking between the trees and up toward the sky while tears fell from my eyes. I'm not exactly sure if I understood what I was doing, but after a few minutes I felt better and climbed back inside, got into bed, and fell off to sleep.

I felt His presence there, and I was comforted and at peace. Now that I'm a little older, I realize that I was surrendering my heart to God in the purest way I knew how, and those acts of submission were helping me press my way beyond the veil. Later along my journey, I stopped visiting that place with Him. I stopped talking to God and my parents and distanced myself from them once the pain began to pile up. I shut down from dealing with hurt feelings and from anyone I thought caused them. With my permission, guilt and shame drove a wedge between me and those who were most important to me.

***

Our famous, historic, first couple had firsthand experience with this struggle. When Adam and Eve were confronted with their wrongdoing, they blamed each other and God instead of coming clean and asking for forgiveness. The guilt and shame caused them to lie and moved them from a place of purity to shame and from innocence to blame. I learned from their story that although God punished them, His love compelled Him to cover them. There are consequences for disobedience, but we don't have to serve a life sentence or end up on death row. Repentance is the way to avoid destruction, and it disarms the enemy and seals off his access to us.

Words, whether written or spoken, held great value for me. They were agreements and promises but were now altered with a clause in tiny microscopic print that read, "I do not intend to hold up my end unless you honor yours."

Aren't we glad God doesn't love the way we do? His love is limitless and always abounding. He is the total and complete fulfillment of "love never fails," a lesson well learned as time passed on, with a fair share of twists and turns to help me evolve.

Bruised and Abused

One summer, my cousin, Derick, who was twenty years old, came up from Texas to visit with us. Late one night after we all retired for the evening, he made his way into my room and slipped his hands underneath my bedclothes. I awakened startled from my sleep and realized my pajamas had been pulled up, and I felt his hands touching my uncovered body. Immediately, I slapped his hands away, but he insisted upon groping me. I continued to resist until he finally got the message and left my room.

My aunt Jackie, on the other hand, was awake in the bed across the room and witnessed what took place. The next morning, she took the matter to my mother and informed her of the incident. Then the interrogation, in its entirety, began and ended with one question. My aunt inquired clumsily, *"Kimberly, did you know he was there?"*

I thought to myself, of course I knew he was there after I woke up with him all over me. No one asked if I was okay. It was as if I was being accused and needed to defend myself or had brought this upon myself in some way. While the question mulled over in my mind, I thought of a few of my own. *Why didn't you scare him off, Aunt Jackie, or yell out or make any noise? Why did you keep silent and just lay there watching?*

Needless to say, this rebuttal took place within, but even more tragic was the perceived threat to my ability to trust. Weren't they supposed to be on my side? Didn't his actions warrant consequence? Shouldn't they have issued him a one-way ticket back to Texas? I was honest about what happened to me that evening, yet, somehow, I felt like the offender instead of the victim. Being made afraid in my own home, the place where I was supposed to find safety and peace, wasn't an option for me.

As a result, I started to distance myself from the people I cared for the most and erected a wall to protect myself. I never actually hated anyone before, but I experienced deep-rooted feelings of detest for my cousin who crossed the line and violated my personal boundary. I also held him personally responsible for turning the place I called home – where I grew up – into an unfamiliar domicile.

I started hanging out a little later than usual to avoid possibly being left alone in the house in case Derick was around. There was a parking lot down the street from 426, where we rode our bikes and hung out until the street lamps came on. I lingered behind a little longer and found some solace with my friends in the neighborhood and their brothers. I was forced to create safe scenarios for myself since it was obvious that I couldn't rely on anyone else to do so.

The incident with Derick seemed to have been swept under the rug. If not, it wasn't common knowledge that he was ever confronted. Besides, he remained with us for the rest of the summer. At fifteen years of age, how was I expected to process what took place?

Even his presence at family gatherings became quite awkward. I wouldn't even look at him. On occasion, he had the nerve to speak and greet me. *"Hi Kim,"* he said, as if he expected a response. I always made sure that the length of time spent in the same room with him, even when other people were around, remained inside of five minutes. I couldn't stand him and what he did was unforgivable. Everyone else enjoyed themselves, while I felt like I was suffocating.

Ironically, my mother and I *did* have "the talk." You know, the one about not allowing people to touch you in places they shouldn't. Weren't there supposed to be consequences if they tried? Imagine my confusion. Nothing is what happened in my situation, absolutely nothing. Everyone else moved on as if it never happened, but I still felt violated. I felt he should have at least been sent packing, yet he was allowed to stay. My difficulty handling what took place sent me in search of ways to guarantee my own safety. My room, once viewed as my sanctuary of solace, my place of retreat, was now a crime scene in my mind. I stayed away as much as possible and resorted to sneaking out to chill with family or friends, and on occasion, I visited with guys I knew even though it wasn't proper. We were just friends and nothing physical was going on. I experienced a great degree of comfort from just being around them.

If there were no consequences to my cousin's behavior, what if it happened again? What if something worse happened? In my mind, next was an option. I needed to hide out just in case while pretending to be unscathed by what already occurred. Now, because the natural course of my young adolescent growth and development was altered, I was wounded and broken and hiding even from what had not happened yet.

That was it, end of story. My cousin wasn't even reprimanded. When summer was over, He was awarded a one-way ticket back to Texas, but not before he impaled me and left behind invisible scars along with feelings of being violated.

***

I never understood why a person became promiscuous or resorted to using drugs or alcohol after they were abused. Why abuse themselves willfully? Maybe the hurt became justifiable if you were, in some way, in control of what happened to you. I never understood soul ties and strongholds either, for that matter, but that best explains what happened. Strongholds were formed, and I became deceived to believe that I was in control and everything was just fine. The pattern of abusive relationships emerged because I was abused and bruised. Now it's much clearer to me why victims transfer or repeat those destructive patterns.

***

At times, I wished I could reside in an alternate reality, a place where everything was unchanged and maintained perfect order. The life I was forced to live was not my own somehow. I wanted to go back, to return to my utopia, but instead, matters only seemed to just get worse.

I heard stories about girls who went out just for fun and never imagined that a night of innocent enjoyment could end tragically even amongst friends. Being raped or molested by someone in your immediate peer circle is not something one considers unless it happens – until it happens.

I have a friend name Lia who shared a very personal situation that happened to her one summer when she vacationed with her cousin Rebeka. They were both sixteen years of age at the time and were trusted to be at home unchaperoned. Lia and Rebeka had just finished dinner and watching a movie, but they were bored. Rebeka's parents were at work, so she decided to call a boy she knew from school. Lia was not privy to the entire conversation but watched as Rebeka laughed and gestured and looked Lia's way occasionally while she chatted on the phone. Before long, Rebeka motioned for Lia to come along. They got in the car and headed off to meet her friends. Lia felt uneasy about the whole situation and couldn't shake that gnawing feeling that suggested they should turn around and go back.

Since Lia was visiting with family, she wasn't familiar with the area and couldn't even get out and catch a cab if she wanted to. She couldn't even describe the house very well, but she told me it was indeed a night she'd always remember.

She continued retelling the events of that evening. After they arrived, she really wanted to leave but kept silent for fear of sounding like a baby. Truth is that she was very young and had no experience whatsoever with sneaking off to meet boys.

High school revealed some very noticeable observations about Lia. She didn't have many friends, and she came off a bit withdrawn and maintained a careful distance from her peers. The few people she took to often stuck up for her and spoke out on her behalf. Although she was obviously uncomfortable, she continued to narrate her story.

She remembered his name, *"Larry Black,"* she whispered. *"He was quite charming,"* she said, *"and was very popular."* He worked very hard to master his game on and off the field. It was evident that he was accustomed to getting his way. As she adjusted her posture and prepared to share the details, I sat on the edge of my seat, listening carefully to her story. For some reason, my eyes became watery, and I fought back the threat of tears.

***

She continued, "At first, everything seemed okay. We were kissing, which seemed quite innocent, and that was something I could handle. I kissed a boy before – it was as far as I ever went with my first love, but this guy was not him. Things went south very quickly, and the dimmed lights in the room grew darker and darker. He laid me back on the bed, and I tried to get up. He wrapped one arm around my small frame to keep me from moving while I struggled to get free from his grip. Tears poured from my eyes and down my cheeks, and I screamed and fought. His expression was a bit sinister, and there was no acknowledgment of my resistance.

My body went limp beneath him, and I looked up into the ceiling and prayed and asked God to allow me to leave my body so I didn't have to live through that night. I wanted to die right there beneath Larry's heavy body. When he was done, he returned to his friends, as if what took place was a normal occurrence.

The reality of my virginity being lost to Larry Black in such a manner left me speechless. I believed my first time was supposed to be special, but that night was far from it – memorable, but not special. There were no I love yous, no flowers, and no one there responded to my cry for help, and... (long pause) there was no answer from God. I felt so abandoned. My cousin and her friends were right outside the door, and no one came in. I wanted to cry on the way back to my aunt's house, but I didn't."

***

I considered Lia a close friend, and there weren't many secrets between us. She was so brave for sharing her story. At a young age, she displayed great courage while I sat in silence with tears streaming down my face, nursing my secret, petrified to utter the words that screamed inside, *"It happened to me too, Lia, and he got away."*

We both cried and held on to each other. Deep down inside, she knew that something bad had happened to me but respected my right to privacy regarding the matter. Over the years, she noticed subtle changes in my behavior and also in my appearance. The group she attended taught her many of the telltale signs, so she was very careful not to offend or implicate me while she shared her story. She knew I wasn't ready to admit to my own trauma but shared hers, hoping I would let someone in.

Hearing Lia's story jarred my memory, and I recalled my own incident. It was as if her account poured salt on open wounds that I neatly dressed with secrecy and silence. In Lia's case, his name was Larry Black, but the guilty-as-charged in my account went by the name Eric Evans, high school star basketball player extraordinaire. The resemblance in our stories was quite unnerving. Now what was once a stifled and repressed memory came clearly into view, and I was reliving every moment of it through the details of her account...

***

I remember standing in the bathroom alone, afraid and trembling. I was undressed and could feel the cold tiles beneath my bare feet. Tears flowed as I tried to drown out the sound of my own whimpers with the noise of the water running from the faucet. I attempted to scrub away every inch of residue that remained on my body until my hands became sore and turned red from my efforts. What I could not remove was the stain of what happened that evening. While hidden behind the locked bathroom door, my secret was safe with me. In an effort to erase any trace of what took place from my memory, I began to pretend that the horrific event never occurred.

"Where did I go wrong? Why was this happening?" I asked myself repeatedly while I listened to the piercing silence that was broken by what I believe was the sound of my tears hitting the tiles on the bathroom floor. I stood there trying to break free from the frozen glare of the reflection of the person I no longer recognized staring back at me from the mirror. Right at that moment, I wanted to check out – first the incident with my cousin, Derick, now this?

I needed to pull myself together, so I proceeded with a great pep talk, but instead, the voice of condemnation echoed back from within. "You just had to mess up, didn't you? Why did you even go to a place like that? You should have just stayed home. It's your fault, you know?" It was my fault, at least I believed that it was. I allowed Eric to steal something very precious – my innocence – and he got away with it. He got away scot-free, and I somehow became the guilty party, and this too became another secret I safely tucked away.

***

As time went on, I replayed and believed the stories I made up about myself. Unlike Lia, I just could not admit what took place that night. Whose story was this, and why was it playing out repeatedly in my mind? Surely, I didn't endure such a horrific experience – at least, that's what I told myself over and over and over. The battle against the voice of condemnation that reminded me that I shouldn't have been there in the first place convinced me all the more that I deserved what happened to me. More importantly, I knew I had to keep this scenario hidden, but the self-condemnation continued – *it was your fault, your fault* – the taunting words to which I often fell asleep and awakened to day after day.

Every day I was ridden with guilt and shame. I became my own judge and jury and convicted myself of a crime I did not commit. I went without eating and replaced food with alcohol to numb the pain. Depression loomed, and I spent a great deal of time crying alone. I had mood swings that ranged from small frustrations to becoming fully enraged over the minutest things. Everything was magnified, and self-control was absent, leaving my emotions to problem-solve. I acted out horribly, and my behavior became justifiable based on the secrets and lies I told myself. I projected a lot of anger toward people and situations that had absolutely nothing to do with what was responsible for my outbursts.

I remained unwilling to verbalize any outward admission, so I internalized and covered my hurt and abuse. I sought out relationships that helped protect my secrets, but what followed as a result, only paid it forward for what was far worse. Although I thought I successfully managed to hide yet another secret, what I didn't realize was that what was on the inside started to display itself outwardly, and my attempts at secrecy failed miserably. The lingering residue of unresolved issues delivered an altered reality and pressed out the mold of an imposter – the person I *thought* I was destined to become by way of incident.

I gave myself quite a few good old talking-tos instead of talking about what I was carrying around, i.e., the broken pieces and fragments of what remained after my innocence was torn away.

I searched for love, but only the kind with limits and conditions would do; anything else was uncontrollable. I stopped looking for God and my path became obscured.

***

If I had come clean, a lot of hurt and collateral damage could have been avoided. Because I was angry and kindled the pain through the secrets I kept, I lashed out when I was unable to maintain the image of the smooth and perfect world I aimed to upkeep. I pushed away anyone who tried to get close for fear of what they would discover.

I couldn't risk picking up the pen, for it too posed a threat to expose what was so well concealed. I lost my desire to speak even through my writing. Though much had occurred, what was at jeopardy was everyone finding out everything. My pen was also an instrument of transparency, and if I commenced with my writing, I had to expose the secrets I held on to and reveal my most vulnerable thoughts. I also ran the risk of being open enough to be hurt again.

Ultimately, I ventured down that dark and dreary road of guilt and shame accompanied by an inability to forgive others and myself. God wanted my heart and the things hidden within it. I was just not able to give it at that time. Imagine trying to hide from God. How ironic, when He knew EVERYTHING, including all I would go through. Nurturing my pain became as natural as breathing, and I had no healthy outlet to speak freely about sexual misconduct, rape, and molestation. For a very long time, I wished bad outcomes for Derick as a result of what he did to me when I was fifteen years old. Oh, and not to mention, the rape – that taboo subject, because mentally it never happened. Whenever the thought of it broke out from its well-secured hiding place, I quickly forced it out of my mind and locked it safely away. I was broken, bruised, and abused. You know the feeling of being alone even in a crowded room? Well, that was every single solitary day for me for a very long time. I thought I could fit back into my world. Instead, I was drowning – kicking and flailing my arms, trying to grab hold to a stable surface before going completely under.

I'm really glad that my attempts to push my family away weren't well-executed ones. They knew something was awry by my unexplained outbursts and that I needed to be rescued; they just didn't know from what. They must have experienced pain as a result of my own.

Parents are most often aware when their children are hurting and are greatly affected by their pain.

So much was damaged, even lost. There was even the tucked-away resentment toward the first man I ever encountered in my life – my father. Forty years later and during an argument no less, I accused him of not caring about me and scolded him for letting Derick stay after he violated me. Much to my surprise, my father was not made aware of what happened. Speaking out would have brought things out in the open and could have prevented some of the poor outcomes.

***

Transition Troubles

Time progressed, and it's true that it waits for no one. Ready or not, it pressed fast-forward, and it was time for my high school graduation. I was notified that I couldn't walk with my class because I didn't pass the regents exam. I was sentenced to summer school and had to take the test again. Time for another defeatist chat to smooth things over.

"Wow," I thought, "This just keeps getting better. Besides, going to college isn't for everyone. Why should anything good come from this? I messed up way too many times. It's my fault, and I deserve to live this life I'm sentenced to."

It was a Friday afternoon in June, and my graduating class gathered together at the stadium not far from my house, two blocks away to be exact. I could hear the announcer at the stadium, and I knew the festivities were well under way. Staying in the house, tormented by sadness and defeat, was not an option. I decided to hook up with a guy I met a few weeks ago.

I encountered him while I was walking to get something to eat. I was with my older cousin, Tiarra, and she immediately threw up the warning signs regarding him. She said, *"Kimberly, if a man calls for you by making hissing sounds like a snake, do not respond. Those types of men are up to no good and won't treat you with the respect you deserve. If he can't walk over and introduce himself like a gentleman, you keep walking."*

I was no longer the twelve-year-old girl who visited her in Yonkers on weekends and listened to her narratives about life. She often spoke to me about growing up to be a young lady while she braided my hair before she took her children and me to the skating rink or the movies. I felt those things no longer applied. Besides, I was seventeen, and she could no longer tell me what to do. I was old enough and grown enough to make my own choices. On several occasions, my cousin expressed her concern for my welfare. She even called every now and then to tell me when someone she knew spotted me here or there. I shrugged it off because I met someone who could help me move forward and forget my past.

Needless to say, not only did I disregard her warning, complete with advice and instructions, I also ignored the conversation that played over in my own mind. As he walked toward me, my inner alarm rang out to cross the street in the opposite direction, but he was a perfect candidate for my need to escape from the pain I was hiding. This guy was just as broken as I was, but this time, this one came with a price.

Again, I hit the snooze button, disarmed the alarms, and ignored those who tried to help me. Joshua felt safe, not the safe I needed, but the kind of safe that chased away the unwanted reminders buried in my memories. Little did I know that dating him also meant disturbing the secrets I fought so hard to remain hidden. I was so far gone that I was no longer looking for safety and protection amongst those who loved me and had my best interest at heart. The lies felt better and began to take over.

***

Meanwhile, as some of my friends prepared to go off to college, I prepared for summer school. My very first day while the teacher took attendance, she looked over at me and said, *"You don't belong here. You passed the test."*

***

It never dawned on me that I would recall those particular words. Now looking back, she was absolutely correct – I didn't belong there. I didn't belong on the road I was traveling either, but where did I belong? Why was I forcing myself into places that weren't suitable? At some point in our lives, we all await the answer to that question.

***

I walked home in a daze and in utter disbelief that the school administrators had made such a huge mistake and discarded it as if nothing happened; and with not as much as an apology. I missed my graduation with my friends, and they had no regard for how I felt. It reminded me of all the other events in my life where I was violated and mistreated without apology or explanation.

I refused to shed another tear. Crying didn't help; it never had. I transferred that energy into something else. I resorted to anger – not the kind that motivated you work harder and become better but the misdirected kind that led to more trouble. Since the ideal of waiting for love and marriage was stolen from me, I decided to turn to Joshua for comfort. I often visited him at work and waited until he got off so we could be together. At first, I felt uncomfortable trying to fit into his life, his world, but where else was I supposed to go? I felt so alone. Joshua made so many frequent trips in and out of jail for drug charges and related crimes that I started thinking he loved being incarcerated more than being with me.

Residing between two different places was difficult. At 426, love remained no matter how many times I walked out and still waited for my return. Going back home meant letting people in and fully divulging my mess. Three years had already passed and seemed to also be associated with the length of my relationships. This three-year stint with Joshua was now the end of what I perceived as love, but this relationship left me with something I could not keep hidden. I was pregnant with Joshua's son.

I didn't willfully disclose that tidbit of information. My eating habits changed drastically – dinner with cereal on the side was a definite telltale sign. I was eating for two, and that little secret was revealed four months into the pregnancy. My father was the first to suspect, especially as he witnessed my meal menu choices.

Waiting for marriage was not a thought. Because of what transpired, I felt that wasn't an option. My parents were very disappointed. My father expressed how he wanted more for me, and my mother was a workingwoman who never once had to rely on public assistance, but I did.

After my son was born, the initial responses of anger and shame were dissolved, and love and excitement returned. I thought to myself, *Kim, you can make it right*, and took a few steps forward only to be set back a few steps. Although I was doing the right things outwardly, such as working and going to school, my motives weren't honorable, and my heart wasn't healed. My parents had a right to be disappointed, but they didn't withhold their love from me, and they extended the same to my newborn son. I couldn't see that at the time, I was still blinded by my need for approval and validation.

Now a single mother, I was still encouraged to follow through and walk the stage the following year. By that, I mean, my parents insisted that I give them the opportunity to attend my graduation. I felt ashamed because no one knew the truth and having to continuously explain didn't help the matter. I had to swallow my pride while I sought vindication for what happened to me. I followed through and walked with the next graduating class. I didn't attend any classes or participate in any of the formalities. I just showed up ready to walk while my family and our newest addition sat in the audience congratulating me, and they all seemed proud.

***

Validations and Violations

After the birth of my son, I thought I finally found my perfect fit – well, my fit-in – motherhood. Now I no longer stood out but was among other young mothers pushing strollers and collecting public assistance.

***

Instead of public assistance being a temporary resource, it became an effortless way to receive compensation and my new way of hiding. I was quite content for a while, only to be disrupted again by my own inner pain and turmoil that kept crying out for resolve. The ache in my hollow place and the void that needed to be filled tried to convince me to settle permanently in what was only intended as a means to an end.

***

This particular weekend, my parents were away, so I decided to visit Joshua's sister on Saturday afternoon. Shortly after I arrived, Joshua walked in and asked me for ten dollars, probably to fund his habit. Well, I was not feeling the whole you-should-feel-like-it's-okay-to-ask-me-for-money ordeal. I'm not sure if he was oblivious to the fact that I was unemployed or if he conveniently dismissed the fact that I was caring for the child he helped bring into the world. Besides, it was my only ten dollars and he had never given me money for anything, so I flat out said, *"No, Joshua."*

My response sent him into a violent rage. Joshua punched me in the face while I held our child in my arms. Blood splattered everywhere, and my son and I ended up at the emergency room. Joshua disappeared before the authorities arrived but had the nerve to call the emergency room to see if we were all right. The officer took the phone and engaged him in an interesting conversation. From what I overheard, the officer shared that he had a very close relationship with his mother and may have had some sisters or even daughters. What I was able to ascertain was that he shared his strong disapproval with what occurred.

My face was swollen for weeks. I tried to avoid mirrors, but reactions from people who saw me reminded me of just how bad it was. I was officially bruised inside and out. I cried when I looked at my disfigured face and wanted to hide until it was healed – well, at least, the visible contusions. If the outward marks were no longer visible, I wouldn't have to replay the incident mentally or listen to myself recant the story.

***

Remember, if I spoke outwardly, then it became reality and was no longer tucked away in my secret, hidden compartment. What I came to realize about what I perceived to be stolen innocence was that it wasn't really stolen. It still yet remained tucked tightly away, concealed, out of sight, to remain hidden from discovery. It was also muted so that its silence would deter my attention – out of sight, out of mind and hear none, speak none.

***

After the abuse incident, Joshua never had to put his hands on me to exert his power or maintain control over me. It was incredibly difficult to break free from him, and his lies and intimidation tactics reinforced that bondage. I was afraid to leave because he threatened to take me to court and have our son taken away from me. Besides, were would I go? Additionally, I still held on to some ideal of having a lasting relationship. I went from seeking love to searching for whatever or whoever would validate me.

Everyone was watching, so I thought, and I had to get it right; but I was powerless, and everything was spiraling out of control. There was no place for guilt, shame, or mess-ups, but my expectations were unrealistic. What existed at that time had absolutely no potential to produce the outcomes I desired. I was blinded to the truth that the love I gave away was unwelcomed but presented a perfect parallel to what was happening with God and my family. They reached out to touch me with their love, and I rejected their advances.

***

Power and control… handed over because I thought it was the only way I could be protected. I no longer trusted myself or my own judgments. Unknowingly, yet somehow voluntarily, I handed power over my life to someone other than God.

***

Joshua provided very little support financially or emotionally. I never petitioned the legal system to force him to pay into the life he took part in creating. Not advocating for my son and remaining silent when I should have spoken up contributed to my passive aggression. I became frustrated and slowly, yet intentionally, distanced myself from the relationship. I thought it to be better, even easier, to separate while our son was still very young. This sort of relationship scenario was approved among my circle of friends with similar stories.

Joshua and I argued constantly, but he never physically wounded me again. I really should have just made a clean break. Regrettably, as a result, I compromised the welfare of our son. A few months after the hitting incident, I agreed to allow Joshua to spend time with our son. I didn't want to be viewed as one of those women who kept their child away from their father because the relationship did not live up to their expectations.

Almost immediately, that decision proved to be a huge mistake. He obviously was incapable of such responsibility. On the very first occasion, he took our son to his aunt's house and left him behind while he went out and got arrested for doing something illegal. I received a phone call from the police station. It was Joshua, and he proceeded to inform me that he told the arresting officers that he left our son in the house unattended and that I should get to the apartment immediately.

At that time, I lived in Southern Westchester and did not drive. I'm still not quite sure how I traveled three towns away in less than an hour on the bus. Nonetheless, I arrived at the apartment and found my son there alone and soaking wet. I was frightened of losing my child and what my parents would say if they found out about the incident.

Fear and shame swept over me. I was not doing very well at all with the "mother thing." Once again, I had to create a cover story that only reinforced what I already believed to be true. *"It was my fault, again! Why didn't I just listen?"* I whispered to myself.

Listening gave threat to vulnerability and required trust and confidence in the source of the dialogue. Listening, in this instance, meant having to revisit the conversation with my cousin Tiarra long before this ever started. It also meant admitting that she was right and, if I had taken her advice, all of this could have been avoided. No.... I had to do it my way and was still trying to make good out of what was doomed from the beginning.

After I got my son cleaned up, we left the apartment. When the door shut behind us, I never looked back. Maybe I couldn't save myself, but this new life that depended on me gave me enough strength to do what was needed, and that was to walk away. That wasn't the remedy for what was wrong on the inside, but it did help me become more determined to protect the child I was given to care for.

His side of the family rarely ever saw my son again; I couldn't chance it. There was an aunt who tried to keep in touch with him for Christmas, but I didn't even want that kind of interaction because it stirred up way too many memories. I wanted absolutely no reminders of the past; although without it, my son would not have been born. I just had to learn to live with the mess I created, but I knew I had to keep them at a safe distance. My reasons for keeping my son away were valid. I was accountable or his well-being until he was old enough to make his own decisions.

My son's father threatened to sue for custody of our child. When I look back on it now, if the courts had to decide who to award custody, I'm sure they would have deferred to my parents! A case was already made against us – arrests, drugs, abuse – and me, a clueless mom.

***

I allowed mental abuse to continue, to control me and fill me with fear, lies, and doubt. I still had not learned how to deal with pain, and it began with the loss of a loved one at an early age. I just refused to face it and thought I could heal on my own.

Over time, what I practiced as a child turned into habitual behavior. Looking away until it was over became second nature to me, and I did the same with my heart. My ability to love freely had died, and the pain escalated and clouded my judgment.

I refused to sit and have a face-to-face and deal with my past pain. Talking with someone wasn't an option, and my writing had ceased. I managed to hide my issues behind something or someone.

From what I thought I knew about God, I figured He had limits, especially with the things I experienced. He couldn't possibly want to deal with someone who sank so low. How could He forgive me after all I'd done? I ventured out so far; there was no way I could go back. I was not a perfect child to Him or my parents; I sat in hopelessness and despair. Still, I felt something tugging at me...

Everyone I sought protection from left me more vulnerable for the next person. They weren't able to provide what I needed. I wore abuse like a garment and expected my family to cover me, without having to reveal what was really going on. My issues were deep; no man could provide help to the extent I needed, and no man could fix what was broken within. I had to go to God and seek Him wholeheartedly and rend my heart completely.

***

And Baby Makes Three

I was no longer with Joshua, who struggled with addiction – his means of medicating to cover his own issues. I was warned to stay away from him in the first place, but he and I had one thing in common – our brokenness. Joshua could not fix what was broken in me, and I was merely another temporary fix for him.

***

Oh, how deceived I was. I actually thought the only way to right this wrong was to find yet another replacement to fill the void, help conceal my indiscretions, and keep hidden the reality of how badly I messed up. Maybe this time it would be different... Instead, I ran into yet another broken soul.

***

I moved on from Joshua right into the grips of a manipulative dealer named Rodney. I met Rodney at my cousin Sheila's house on the south side. I never really frequented that side of town; however, I started adapting to the loose and fast girl mentality to free myself from the girl who loved wearing dresses and pretended to dance at the ball with prince charming. I wasn't even convinced any more that prince charming ever existed. Even if he did, he wouldn't be interested in what that girl had become.

Besides, good girls had no place in the world. What a stigma! In reality, what side of town you lived on didn't matter one bit. We all had a lot more in common than we would admit. Our brokenness, our insecurities, and what was hidden behind our pretense was evidence of the depth of our pain and our cries for help because we were drowning, and those issues were not bias to upbringing.

Rodney taught me how to steal, even from my own parents. Now I was paying a heftier price for the love, safety, security, and validations I thought I had to obtain from someone else. Rodney told me that he had debts and promised we would replace what was taken. What a huge mistake! My behavior hurt my parents and created distrust between my family and me, but like with any drug, I got hooked on the high. Who was this girl? I barely recognized myself.

I flirted with danger often; being in places I would not have been caught dead in became my new norm. I felt like I was in control, but how, when I was now involved with a man who entertained the company of other women as well? I didn't feel special at all, and my self-worth was just about non-existent. I accepted anything from Rodney and replayed and reiterated the stories to myself he told me to cover and justify his infidelities. Besides, some of something was better than nothing, just as long as I felt like the important one. A sure sign that it was time to move on was when I started fighting off women who he was obviously telling the same stories he told me.

I couldn't live that lie a moment longer. I was most uncomfortable in the life of a man who didn't want just me. I didn't belong, but my secrets held me back from moving forward. Strangely enough, when I mustered up enough gumption to let go, I discovered that I was pregnant again, and another three-year relationship had come to an end. Fortunately, the only thing I walked away from the relationship with was a child. I was thoroughly engaged in Russian roulette – a game of chance – because Rodney was unfaithful and had multiple sex partners.

***

Diseases are not at all familiar with favoritism, and they don't pass by as a result of intimate knowledge of who we are. Who we choose as mates matters because soul ties are formed. The purpose for sexual relations was assigned to marriage. Yes, to procreate, but also to join man and woman as one flesh. Soul ties are very difficult to break free from. What we crave and desire, whether good or bad, has a way of causing us to desire it all the more. Even against our better judgment, we experience a case of the "can't-help-its" because of the soul tie.

I learned that the brain releases a chemical called Dopamine in response to pleasurable stimuli. Dopamine is also present and very much involved in additions and addictive behaviors; increasing the desire to repeat the activity responsible for pleasure – sugar, drugs, sex, etc.

When we are in tune with the Holy Spirit, He will lead and guide us along righteous paths. Our decisions and desires are then guided by the Spirit of truth and not tainted by what we pursue in our flesh.

What I truly desired was love and comfort. Because I had so many unresolved issues, especially hurt and betrayal, I was drawn to people, places, and things that fueled the problem. My flesh didn't protest because it was receiving what was pleasurable through the sexual encounters and a daring lifestyle. The flesh wants what is pleasurable and has no meter for whether it is good or bad. My soul, however, was in jeopardy, and I was still lost and had deep brokenness that was not mended by those habits and behaviors. I had an addiction. I so badly craved to be loved and validated.

Without telling anyone what was going on inside, I kept searching for the next someone or something else that would make it all go away. I changed stations to drown out the sounds and maintain what I thought was control over these situations. Instead of the safety and shelter of love I longed for, I engaged in relationships that further violated me and robbed me of my self-worth and dignity. I wanted to be **vindicated** to erase the guilt and shame I harbored; I wanted to be **validated** and know that I was good enough. If I had only paused long enough to remember that God already fearfully and wonderfully made me.

***

I soon became the mother of two – a son and a daughter – two perfect loves, who looked at me through eyes of unconditional love and had no idea their mother was flawed. All they knew was that I was mom, and to them, that was perfectly fine. Sadly, I had no idea how to give them what they needed. How much of my trash could I transfer on to my children, when I was the one who would influence them? They were so innocent. What I knew for sure was that I didn't want my children to turn out as messed up as I was.

Rodney didn't stick around, and, once again, my parents helped me with another new life I brought into this world. I was scared and felt even more betrayed. Although I put up a good front on the outside, my inward parts told a different story. I knew I wanted something different, but I just didn't think it could happen. My most inner desires were still unfulfilled, and I felt alone.

I was still receiving public assistance, but a desire for change emerged. I kept feeling the need to get up even though I wasn't strong enough to stand as a result of the issues I kept hidden, but I was determined to try my best. The day my phone rang and my cousin spoke with me about an opportunity, I thought just maybe the change in course I needed was possible.

***

Through this, I learned a valuable lesson: that people will treat you according to what you allow. What you believe about yourself is what you will eventually attract. I became a magnet for anyone or anything I thought could provide the love I looked so desperately for, but the scars still remained.

I was great at pretending; I would have done well in theater and film with all the acting I was doing. I moved further and further away from the place called familiar and deeper into the depths of the unfamiliar. I tried to lay hold of the place I once knew before I made so many mistakes. I never wanted to fail my children, who saw nothing but happiness when they looked at me. It was the opposite when I looked at them; what I saw was how much of a disappointment I was to them.

If you believe you are nothing, that's exactly what you are going to get – nothing. Let's be honest, we have all heard the song and saying, "Nothing from nothing leaves nothing." It's universal math;

nothing will change until you begin adding what is of value; then and only then can you expect to yield favorable results.

***

Course Correction

Of course, obstacles, challenges, and hurdles accompany every new accomplishment. People will try and hinder you from reaching your next plateau, almost as if they were assigned the job to do just that. Others will open doors for you and remind you that the rest is up to you.

***

In 2001, I received a call from my cousin, Tiarra, the one who looked out for me when I was a teenager. The same cousin who tried to warn me about Joshua and his type, who I should have listened to when I was 17 but didn't because I was grown and knew everything. Ashamedly, Tiarra, my cousin who I turned my back on, but who never gave up on me.

Tiarra spoke to me about what she called the Clout Program. The program was established and implemented in 1991 and was a joint venture with the Westchester Department of Social Services and Pace University. Clout offered certificates in computer applications followed by internships and employment placement opportunities for enrollees. This was my chance to make it right; just the course correction I needed, equipped with an opportunity to further my education, enhance my skills, and obtain sustainable employment through the pursuit of an associate degree in information technology.

At that time, I worked at CVS, making $7.00 an hour with two children to support. I visited social services and met with my caseworker. I was excited for the chance to get my life together and further my education. I always wanted to work in an office environment, behind a desk, doing something that helped others.

Imagine my extreme disappointment when my caseworker said, *"No, it's too expensive to attend."* What I didn't know was that the program was grant funded and welcomed single mothers with one-year-olds, who were collecting public assistance. I fit the criteria perfectly, but he suggested that I do something else, like nursing. There was nothing wrong with a nursing career; I just knew that it wasn't for me.

When I returned home, I decided to get in touch with the supervisor at social services. I just couldn't shake the feeling that I needed to be a part of that program. In my mind, the program was designed specifically for me, and somehow, they were expecting me to attend. The supervisor picked up on the second ring. She must have been in tune with what I was thinking. She provided me with step-by-step directives on what I needed to do on my end; one of which was to quit my job at CVS at the end of the month and report to social services the next Monday morning to enroll, and I did exactly that.

That Monday morning when I returned to the Department of Social Services, I had no idea that a conversation between my caseworker and his supervisor had already occurred. Obediently, I followed the directions I received prior to that day, and I calmly and politely asked to speak with my caseworker. After waiting a few hours, he called me in, and we both sat down at his desk and made small talk before he asked why I was there. He already knew the answer to that question, but nonetheless I responded, *"I'm here to register and enroll at Pace University."* I wanted to enroll for the fall semester, which began in September.

He took my identification card and went to make copies. After he returned, he couldn't hold off any longer. In fact, it became obvious that he was quite annoyed with me. I realized he must have received a phone call or reprimand from his supervisor. As I signed the papers, I heard him say in a light whisper that was low enough only for him and me to hear but careful enough that no one else around overheard his off-the-cuff remark, *"People are not going to like you going over their head,"* he said in a threatening tone.

My caseworker didn't have a valid reason to deny my participation in the program, and with circumstances in my favor; I saw no reason why I couldn't attend either. This was only the beginning. As a result of opportunities like the Clout Program and in spite of those who sought to hinder my way, I continued on my journey in search of what I was destined to become. Whether I was aware or not, I was well on my way to discovering my purpose, and there was no time to waste arguing with my caseworker about his inappropriate comment. I was EXCITED and COLLEGE-BOUND! I had an overwhelming feeling that I had finally seized a chance to do something right in hopes of finding a job with better pay to support my new family.

***

Every situation we encounter leaves traces and clues toward our purpose. If I allowed what my caseworker told me initially to deter me, I wouldn't be able to declare my own testimony, "Yes, you can overcome!" The only things broken as a result of what presented itself as an obstacle were the chains and shackles of being dependent on government assistance and barely able to afford to take care of my family. However, often what God uses to draw us out may not be our ultimate destination but one of the stops along the way...

***

So, I was finally enrolled in college at Pace University, studying information technology. I loved computers, breaking them down and building them up. I was well on my way to becoming a computer technician or assigned to settle down in a fancy office with a beautiful view.

Strangely, I often found myself advocating for others. It actually became more of a passion that I wasn't initially aware of. Whenever a challenge arose, something on the inside was moved to seek out a solution. If I encountered an obstruction, I knew there was a workaround.

The Clout Program had a strict attendance policy. We weren't allowed to miss too many classes, especially on Saturdays. I was motivated to propose to the administration consideration for a daycare for the mothers in attendance so they weren't forced to drop out because they didn't have babysitters or the ones they had weren't interested in working weekends.

Initially, because of the sense of urgency, they thought the proposal was directly associated with my own personal situation. They were surprised at my level of concern when they learned that it wasn't motivated by my need but the need of other attending moms. Thereafter, they explained to me all the reasons they could not accommodate that request. I had a lot to learn and a long way to go, but I never quit. I knew people achieved their goals; I just didn't know exactly how they got there. Everyone was born with a unique gift to make a difference; it just had to be identified within; then put to good use.

I completed my certificate program at Pace University and was given the honor to deliver the welcome speech at our closing-out ceremony. I remembered feeling both excited and nervous all at the same time. I welcomed the guest commissioner of social services, the president of the program, and our families and friends. I was honored and delighted for the opportunity to speak from my heart and share with all in attendance how very grateful we were for this chance.

I felt great and was motivated to go beyond a certificate, so I took the necessary steps and earned my associate degree. Great changes were taking place and I was transforming. I was nervous in the beginning, but once I found my footing and got in my groove, the energy I felt was as natural as breathing. When it was over, I could hardly believe that I achieved those things.

I will forever be grateful for those opportunities coordinated to occur at those preordained moments in my life. Doors were opened to new beginnings, and the place of hopelessness and despair began to fade away. The pain was disarmed and lay dormant long enough for me to move beyond where I was and where I had been; even baby steps warranted a celebration.

Graduation day came again. The weather was very warm that day as we drove and made our way to the Pace University campus in Pleasantville, NY, for the big day. Because it was so warm, I probably should have made better wardrobe choices beneath my black graduation gown.

My son, who was nine-years-old at the time, asked, *"Mom, how many times will you graduate?"*

I smiled at him and said, *"You and your sister must continue where I leave off,"* in an effort to sow and plant seeds about their future.

When we arrived on the huge campus grounds, I could hardly believe we were there. They had ice-cold bottles of water to keep cool from the heat and shades to help block the sun. My dad parked the car, and my parents and my children went on to secure their seats. I joined up with some of my other graduating classmates, found our places, and waited until they played our song.

Everything was perfect, but my fellow classmates and I still needed a few assurances. We asked the program director if our degrees would display evidence of our social services affiliation, or would we receive the real deal? She reassured us that the only differentiation would be in the degree classifications: associates, bachelors, masters, or doctorate, and that we would march in that order. We were legit – an official part of the 2003 graduating class of Pace University. The certification program initiated through the Department of Social Services was the stepping-stone to the next level of achievement, and I would receive the degree to prove it.

Even to this day, I still carry the pocket-sized degree in my wallet that reads, *"I have completed the prescribed studies and satisfied the requirements for the degree, <u>Associate in Science</u>."* Nowhere did it state how I came to obtain it, what doors I had to venture through to get to it, or the prerequisite drama that got me there. It solely stated the outcome; that I earned *"the rights, privileges, and immunities thereunto appertaining"* – a more decorated way to say that I met the criteria and did all that was required to obtain the degree, and I was qualified to do what it stated.

Although somewhere deep within we were convinced that we were different, and felt somewhat like outsiders, no one associated our degree with where we started. We were never treated like outcasts and were shown a sense of belonging.

It was unheard of for a person with my track record to walk amidst doctors and lawyers. I never imagined that day would forever be impressed in the minds of my children without the need for me to speak a word to inspire them.

An added benefit for my attendance and completion of that program was that if my daughter, who was four years old at the time, decided to attend Pace University, she would receive a legacy award. So, the opportunity afforded me offered generational benefit as well.

One day while I was sitting on the couch in the living room, I overheard my mother talking on the phone about my graduation. Her dialogue implied that she affirmed with whomever she was speaking to on the line that I planned to continue my education and do the coursework to get my bachelor's.

I thought, *Why not?*

So, that September I enrolled into a bachelor's program for a degree in communications at The College of New Rochelle. I was still pretty much content with the way things were, and I didn't need to confront or disclose my secrets. Classes and homework were more than enough to keep me busy and keep those concealed things tucked away. I was working on everything but the internal issues that were still very much a part of my hidden reality.

While in pursuit of my bachelor's degree, I discovered just how much I enjoyed helping others. If I wanted to effectively help other people, I needed to first deal with myself, right? How could I talk about love and healing while my brokenness was obscured by my accomplishments? So, I dodged the idea, and I decided that I wanted to become a sports announcer for a popular radio station in New York City. I had no prior job knowledge or experience, just documents stating that I was a Pace University graduate and an attendee at The College of New Rochelle.

I came up with an impressive course list, completed an internship, and cited as references my son's sports participation. He played community football and little league baseball, but those credentials didn't get me very far, mainly because I didn't know how to use them, but that didn't stop me from trying.

I was drinking the night before I had my interview. The next morning, I got ready, and me and my I'm-the-boss-already attitude took a cab from Westchester to New York City. Aside from being nervous, I had a terrible cold and was completely unprepared. I could barely read the words from the script they provided, and needless to say, I never received a call back.

You see, I attempted to trade and exchange God's plan, which had its own set of requirements, for worldly treasures and outward accomplishments. Because it was what I orchestrated and outside of God's will, the outcome was thwarted. I was still very immature in so many ways. If it was what God intended it, He would have prepared me ahead of time, and the door would have been opened. Besides, I was still drinking, one of the habits I picked up in my loose and fast days, and it was getting worse.

***

Father knows best, period! He is the One who determines the appropriate time for every blessing. His NO is also a blessing, often for reasons unknown to us. It could be that potential harm would come to us, or perhaps He has better and more for us. In my case, there were parts of the process I could not forego. Although I was advancing and achieving goals, I had not resolved my personal conflicts, and bruises and wounds were still not healed.

I was still longing for a relationship that would right my wrongs and provide my children with a father I felt they deserved. Life as a single parent wasn't what I saw for myself, and the constant question from my children as to why their fathers didn't want them perpetuated hate, guilt, and sadness. I associated more with my sense of failure and inadequacy than my short roster of accomplishments.

Old feelings crept in and familiar scenes reemerged, especially when I started clubbing with my cousins and friends. The world still had a hook in me, and I was not yet aware of the strength on the inside of me to fight against such temptation. Drinking and unresolved matters produced a lethal cocktail. While the people I associated with were social sippers, I drank to suppress what was going on inwardly.

Again, I was in another vicious cycle, and each phase of the storm became more fierce and the whirlwind romances even more destructive. This one was more dangerous than the last. Why? Well, he wore a convincing costume – well-dressed and educated but dark, and not his skin complexion. God used this relationship to bring me face to face with His divine presence and my own depravity. The voice of God grew louder and louder; instead of listening, I was intentional about my own agenda – to move beyond the three-year relationship marker, which I thought increased my chance of success…

***

In Walks Mr. Perfect

I secured Section 8 housing and moved into my own apartment. I was working toward completing my undergraduate degree and employed with a medical company as a data entry operator. I was feeling pretty good about my accomplishments and new-found independence. This was supposed to be a happy time, but I made it as far as my last semester when depression kicked in and I stopped attending college.

I wasn't able to shoulder the burden any longer, but I didn't know how to let go. Often, I sat on the floor in my apartment in the dark, drinking, crying, and yelling. My breakdowns were sporadic, and the feelings of failure crept back in. I was at odds with my family, and they had no idea what was wrong with me, but they knew I needed help. I argued with those who loved me about past issues they knew nothing about.

I left my children with their grandparents often to avoid them witnessing my poor behavior. I tried to manage my drinking by only indulging on weekends, but it quickly spilled over into the week, and I became consumed by it. Sometimes I drank until I passed out.

So, what brought this on? I attributed all of it to years of lugging around hurt, shame, guilt, betrayal, violations through rape and molestation, and every baggage item that I refused to acknowledge as such. Although, somehow, wherever I went, there they were. With nowhere to turn, I became even more determined not to let my guard down ever again. I was running from myself and chasing myself at the same time and didn't know if I was coming or going. My thoughts said that it was entirely my fault, but I was determined to prove them wrong.

One evening, while out partying, I met a dark, handsome stranger. He wore sunglasses, so I couldn't see his eyes, but his body was built up nicely, like a bouncer, and he seemed perfect.

***

For the life of me, I never understood why people wore shades in the club. If eyes were supposed to be windows to the soul, then why the desperate attempt to hide them? Why keep a window covered in a place that is dark already? How could I judge someone else for doing exactly what I was doing? No matter how well I changed it up on the outside, I still managed to attract the same kind of people. It's as if they had a unique ability to sniff out my weaknesses, vulnerabilities, and low self-worth. Unresolved issues were the magnets that attracted wrong things; in my case, wrong people... again!

***

Now, in walks Leo, a.k.a. *Mr. Perfect*. He apparently believed himself to be God's gift to women – a prized catch no less. Leo had a way of helping you while at the same time convincing you that your life would be lacking without him. For a time, I believed the hype. What Leo represented was the mirror image of my own well-dressed chaos.

He took my children and me shopping and helped around the apartment. He also rearranged my closet according to a color-code system; he cleaned and organized my refrigerator and arranged the cabinets so that all the labels always faced forward. I watched him become my Mr. Fixit, while he put my life in order. Oh, I almost forgot to mention that he kept me in ample supply of libations; you know, the alcohol kind. He seemed to be the missing piece to make the picture complete without any change requirement on my part. Leo was very methodical; everything in its place. I thought about the movie, *Sleeping with the Enemy*, but I laughed it off and told myself I was just being silly.

Why, why, why would that particular movie come to mind? Why did I dismiss it? Why would I even equate him with that *type of character?*

***

Leo encouraged me to go back to school, and he dropped me off and picked me up when I had classes. At first, I thought nothing of it until I saw him outside my classroom one day. Perhaps he just came early, I thought to myself, but that was only the beginning. I started connecting the dots and became more aware of a particular pattern that was emerging. There was more going on beyond the obsessive-compulsive behavioral displays around the house.

***

I believe God was trying to get my attention, to open my eyes, but I didn't trust Him – God, yes God. I pointed the finger at Him for all the issues that plagued my life. If He loved me, why did He allow me to endure all of those traumatic experiences? The war continued; there was a fight for my heart, and my knack for shutting out the uncomfortable started to work against me.

My own inability to process hurtful emotions landed me in some precarious situations. Although I couldn't see it, everyone else could. No matter how much I pretended, no one believed me, and my family and friends were very much afraid for me. My eyes weren't quite yet affixed on how I was playing with danger.

***

One day in the car, I mentioned to Leo that I dated guys bigger than he. Oddly, his response was, *"Kimberly, that's not right. Why would you say that to me? Makes me feel like you're using me or something."*

After I said it and he responded, I realized there was something wrong with that. What was *my* motive? We both wanted control over the relationship, but how was that possible when neither would submit? He actually told me that his ex-wife and child were afraid of him and about how he put his hands on her and felt he had a right to do so because he was her husband. That should have been alarming. Concernedly, I was really out of touch and still had no sense of danger.

Somehow, I managed to actually complete my undergraduate coursework and get my degree. This time, I walked the stage at Rockefeller Center. I felt like I lived in contradiction and duplicity. How was it that I earned degrees and took classes in sociology and psychology and still missed all the obvious warning signs in my personal life? How could a woman function professionally in public and still remain empty and broken in private?

The pain grew worse. I continued to drink to drown out the sorrow. The alcohol served as a sedative, and my night cries and outbursts only subsided when I finally drifted off to sleep. I called for God, but He didn't seem to answer anymore. I no longer wanted to feel the way I did. I went from medicating my brokenness only at night to full-blown inebriation on the weekends. The alcohol was the only thing that brought me any degree of satisfaction. Was I an alcoholic? Of course not! I never used uncomfortable labels, because I would then become accountable. The true answer was, YES, I was an alcoholic… big time.

My lifestyle even distanced me from my best friend, especially after she confronted me about Leo and my drinking. She flat out told me in no uncertain terms, *"Since this new relationship, your drinking has gotten worse."* I immediately became angry at her; not because what she said wasn't true, but because I did not want to face up to her disapproval of my man and my drinking. I responded by putting space between us. Besides, Leo made me feel he was for me and that everyone else had it out for me.

Everyone, including my children, disliked Leo. He even said to me one day, *"Your children aren't afraid of me."*

I responded defensively and said, *"And they are not going to be."*

He had the audacity to test out his theory one night when he yelled at them and ordered them to sleep. I walked in and threw a bottle aimed straight for his head, but I missed. He crossed a dangerous line with my children. Although the little girl within me wasn't protected, I vowed that my children would be.

That display of rage didn't begin with Leo; it was brewing down on the inside and developed over time. The incident with my children was the perfect opportunity for it to unleash itself. How foolish was I to believe that I could win everyone over and keep peace between both sides as long as everyone stayed away from the doors in my life marked "off limits?" I even did my best to appease Leo by doing everything just as he would have it to reassure him that I wasn't nor had any intention of cheating on him, but he constantly accused me anyhow.

I never had many of the men I dated around my children; in fact, my daughter was five when I started seeing Mr. Perfect, and he was the only man she knew who wasn't her father. My son only ever met two of the men in my life. I didn't want to have a revolving door of men walking in and out of my children's lives, so I was overly invested in making this relationship work. Leo was 11 years my senior and had more life experience. I became comfortable with him caring for me and slowly allowed him to assume control. I no longer had the upper hand. I'm not sure I ever did, but Mr. Perfect was in complete control, right down to the clothes I wore.

***

Careful... careful... You see, the thief comes to steal your purpose, kill your joy, and destroy your future.[2] *Whenever I tried to do well, someone or something was always there to remind me of my past and reinforce my inability to change. In this case, Leo, Mr. Perfect, was that someone, and he became even more strategic with his insanity.*

***

I was never afraid of Leo, but other people were afraid for me. He always accused me of cheating on him, and he insisted upon choosing my attire. I couldn't be overly dressed for work because somehow it translated into me meeting up with someone. I couldn't take the train because of some bizarre excuse about a former train-related incident. Later, I discovered the real reason he was so paranoid was to avoid me running into the other girl he was seeing. Most often where suspicions reside, there is also guilt and a supported hidden agenda.

Although I could no longer ignore the warning signs, I felt stuck. Mr. Perfect even told me one day to my face, *"You'll do anything just to have a boyfriend."* He was right, and at that point, he was there solely out of convenience. Regardless of how awful we treated one another, the situation wasn't fair to either of us. We both had way too many unresolved issues.

---
[2] John 10:10 paraphrased

Leo usually spent weekends with me while my children stayed with their grandparents. They were usually quite content, especially when their cousins were visiting.

One day, while at my parents' home at 426, Leo fell asleep on the couch on the second floor. I went upstairs to the third floor where there were two bedrooms and a living room that extended into a huge play area for the growing grandboys who played harder than the girls. An hour later, Leo came up with a disturbed and worried look on his face. He grabbed hold of my arm and asked, *"Kim, please promise to never leave me. Say you'll stay by my side."* I'm not sure what sort of dream he had, but I saw him through a different pair of lenses.

We left my parents' home and headed back to my place. All I could think about were those words and the way he gripped my arm. We pulled up in front of my apartment, and I turned to look at him while he was talking. I felt numb; as blank as his expression behind the shades he wore when we first met at the club. For some reason, I realized that there was a darkness behind the eyes I looked into for the past three years, and fear gripped me. I thought to myself, *"How did he find me? Where did he come from?"*

When I finally spoke, I asked him to take me back to my parents' house, and he did. I got out of the car, went into the house, closed the door, and proceeded up to the third floor. I watched him from the window until he finally drove off. *"Well, what was that?"* I thought. I believe it became obvious that something was about to interfere with the world I created that would let me know for certain that I was definitely not in control.

I recalled another dream instance where I woke Leo up in the middle of the night. When I opened my eyes, he asked if I was okay. He said that I made noises and motioned as if I was trying to get away from someone or something. He said, *"I wanted to save you, but I couldn't. I wasn't sure if I should wake you up."* My coping strategies were failing, and I didn't know how to handle the fact that the segmented worlds I created were colliding and nothing was as neatly arranged as I thought.

***

Outwardly, I was accomplishing things, but inwardly, I was dying spiritually. Drinking for me became as natural as breathing. One night, Leo took a picture of me at a club. I was inebriated – passed out. My mess had finally gotten the best of me. My limp body was slumped lifelessly across the couch, and I looked as if I were dead.

I became angry about the photo because it threatened to call me into accountability and face the truth about myself. The picture wasn't guilty of anything; it only captured a snapshot of the truth. More accurately, I was really angry at my own reality and the revelation that if I kept going, I was surely bound to die.

Besides, who was he to point out my issues? How could he criticize while he was the source of my supply? Was it just *him* or was I equally accountable?

***

Ironically, one day during an argument, Mr. Perfect screamed, *"You need to GO TO CHURCH!"* It was at that particular moment that I heard Him; not Leo, but God, my Father. Since I wasn't listening to anyone else who truly loved me, God used Leo to lead me back to Him. As a result, I attended services occasionally at first. I even sought out different places to fellowship to avoid attending the congregation where I grew up. That was too much like going back home where everyone knew who I was before my worldly encounters.

Soon thereafter, the relationship between Leo and me changed drastically. His grip was loosening, and the one God had on me became stronger. Although I didn't recognize much of a difference, Mr. Perfect did and expressed his disapproval. He said, *"You are no fun anymore. I don't think you should go back to church."*

Then Leo, the same guy who sought to guilt and shame me and told me I needed to go back to church, brought over a huge bottle to corroborate his account and prove just how weak I was. He conveniently admitted that he made a mistake and that my decision to go back to church was the wrong one.

A few months later, I was diagnosed with an overactive thyroid. I went from a whopping 125 pounds down to 105. Walking from the living room to the kitchen felt like a mini marathon and my throat burned when I tried to drink. I thought with all my asking, *"Wasn't there an easier way of getting me to let go of drinking?"*

Because of the iodine treatments, I was confined to my apartment for a few days, eating out of paper plates and drinking out of plastic cups. I made sure I properly discarded the disposable items and washed and wiped down everything I handled.

I fell back into fear of being vulnerable, but my family was there again, of course, to pick up the pieces. I couldn't help but feel extremely guilty for how I treated them. Reality stared me directly in the face, and I didn't want to be alone. I decided I wanted Leo back, but he ignored my calls. That wasn't uncommon when I didn't do what he asked. He called himself punishing me or putting me in time out by staying away. Go figure, I was a grown woman who consented to such behavior because I wanted a relationship. Sure, it was far from perfect, but I wanted it. I wanted back the trust and confidence I once felt as a little girl – like the certainty of the car pulling in the driveway at 3:30pm sharp every day. After days went by with no response from Leo, I stopped calling, and I assumed we were officially broken up. There was no contact between us, no more rants on his voicemail, and no more blowing up his phone.

This segued to the perfect quiet storm. One night, my cousin and I shared movie night over the phone. She lived in New Jersey, so we had a conference call and watched *Madea's Family Reunion* together from our separate living rooms. While we laughed and sipped our wine, I heard someone fumbling with the keys at my front door. At first, I thought maybe my son had accidently dropped his keys, but almost immediately, I sensed something was amiss.

I got up and walked toward the door slowly; then I saw him. It was Leo. My mind raced to the thought about how ex's return in a fit of jealous rage. I knew something wasn't right, and I didn't hit snooze this time.

When he finally got the door opened and ran through my apartment into the bedroom, I hung up on my cousin and ran out of the house. Later, she told me how scared she was because she heard the ruckus but didn't know what was happening. There was actually a domestic violence scene in the movie we were watching, which seemed to play out in real time.

I ran as fast and as far away as I could and called the police. I told them what was happening, but he was right behind me in hot pursuit. The police started asking way too many questions, so I hung up on them so I could avoid Leo. The police called back repeatedly, but I was too afraid to answer. By that time, we both stood on the corner, and two cop cars rode past us with lights flashing and sirens blaring. They stopped right in front of my apartment. I walked back toward my place, and Leo followed close behind. What was at best a two-minute walk felt more like fifteen minutes, and in slow motion no less. Neighbors stood outside, and parents from the daycare in the area were also watching. Everyone stood around, and I held my breath in fear of what might have happened before I finally reached the crowd of onlookers. I stopped in front of my home, and an officer asked, *"Ma'am, did you call 911?"* At that moment, I collapsed and broke out in tears. Everything I was holding in spilled out right in front of everyone.

The officers placed Leo in the patrol car, and two other officers walked me inside. I sat down on the couch. I was emotionally drained. I began to wonder if I overreacted by following my first instinct. The police had already questioned the neighbors and the tenants in the downstairs apartment, who were picking up their children. They pretty much had most of the story, but they still needed me to corroborate the account. The officers informed me that the landlady's mother gave Leo the keys. She wasn't aware that we were no longer together. He told her and the officers that he was concerned because he hadn't heard from me. I guess I was supposed to believe that he never received the slew of phone calls and messages I left on his voicemail before I stopped calling.

The scenario was quite odd. I heard the officers talking to me, but it was as if I wasn't present. I just wanted everyone to leave so that night would be over. They knew I was covering up by the way I spoke, and they weren't buying it. When I began to second-guess myself, the officers explained that my actions were justified. I, on the other hand, was no longer in control, and the door to my secrets was flung wide open, and everything I tried to hide was exposed. There was no more pretending that I was okay. I made another attempt to hide when my son came in and asked, *"Mom, are you alright?"* I responded, *"Yes,"* like it was a normal everyday occurrence for us to have police officers standing in our living room. I put forth every effort to never let anyone see me weak or afraid. Now, I was becoming undone.

***

I kept up a façade for quite a long time – at least I thought so. I ignored all the bells and whistles and questioned if I was even in real danger. The answer was YES! YES! YES! YES! The danger started with me. For years, I battled within¬ – a virtual tug-of-war ensued and assumed many casualties, including my family and friends. I am so grateful that those relationships were stronger than what I was going through. In most cited cases, mental and emotional abuse almost always preceded physical abuse along with depression, a byproduct of all of the abuse. I believed all the lies I told myself and listened to the wrong narrative about who I was and whose I was. I was deluded to believe that my mess was neatly contained and packed away. I wanted help without judgment and forfeited out of fear that I wouldn't get it.

Help

Weeks following the incident, I had an appointment to speak with someone from the Victims Unit. Before I went, I called the police station and asked about Leo. I still wasn't sure if what happened really took place. I continued with my inquiry, and the woman on the phone kindly put things in perspective. She simply told me that if I wasn't in any danger, I wouldn't have run or called the police and that the first instinct is usually the correct one. She went on to share that I should never have hung up the phone and in the event of such an unfortunate incident, to safely tuck the phone away so they could track my location.

Still in a daze, I walked down to the precinct. I felt very uncomfortable sitting in the Victims Unit. My mind still fought the idea of me being a victim of anything. That would imply that I was weak. Oh, I was quite the stubborn one, still protecting the wounded little girl inside who trusted absolutely no one.

There were two professionals in the office to assist me; and after speaking with them for 20 minutes, I declined any future help. They were still talking as I rushed and gathered together my belongings. They asked, *"Why are you refusing help?"* No longer careful for my word choices, I told them, *"I am not sure what took place or if what I thought about that evening was real."* The truth is, they were headed somewhere I wasn't exactly ready for them to go, and what they already knew was more than enough.

***

Emotional abuse didn't leave visible scars. It only reinforced the negative inferences I rehearsed about myself. I was blinded to how much damage I was causing by keeping things inside.

I went back to life as usual and tried to collect the pieces and place them behind a more secure door. This time, I was unsuccessful. It was too late. No one, and I mean no one, was buying my I'm good and I'm fine stories any longer. I was still that 14-year-old, vulnerable, little girl who didn't feel protected in her own home. At age 35, I could no longer protect her by keeping her locked away, reliving everything that happened to her.

***

The letter arrived from the court and stated that both Leo and I had to appear before the judge. The court date came, and I went on my own because I refused to tell anyone else about what happened. When I arrived, I was instructed to wait in the district attorney's office. I took a seat and waited patiently until it was time to see him. I experienced a host of mixed feelings while I waited to be called. It took an unusually long time for our case. In the meantime, I talked with plain-clothes officers – just conversation, and I made certain to stick to my script about the details of the incident.

Another hour passed, when someone walked in and said I was free to go. I was a bit confused and wondered why no one called me. They knew the truth, and covering it up was no longer an option. One of the officers walked in talking, unaware that I was still in the room. Disgusted, he recanted, *"The guy said that he was willing to give her space because he loves her."* Go figure. He halted almost in mid-sentence when he looked over and discovered that I was still there. The entire office became so quiet, you could hear a pin drop.

***

Leo, aka Mr. Perfect, was far from perfect for me. He validated me and made me feel that I wasn't broken. Though we drank, partied, and argued, he allowed me to believe there was nothing wrong with me, so I exchanged control over my life to be confirmed by him. He also almost succeeded at severing any connections I had with my family or friends. Other close relationships intimidated him and interfered with his plan. My soul was so intertwined with his that it was difficult to let go. Even though I knew he was no good for me, the severing was still painful, like the gnawing away at the threads of the cords that bound us together.

***

That day, the justice system protected me from myself, and I was kept from changing my mind and recanting my story. An order of protection was executed, and both of our signatures were required on the official paperwork. The police department couldn't risk not treating this seriously because not long before my incident, an intruder murdered a young girl I was acquainted with growing up.

I didn't see Leo leave the courtroom, nor did I encounter him while I waited in the hallway for the elevator to leave. I left the courthouse and walked back home. I was numb and had no idea what to do next. The only thing that came to mind was to drink, and I did until I fell asleep in my own tears.

***

The order of protection I took out against Mr. Perfect expired in 2014. From the time it was issued until then, a lot had taken place in my life. I became a little stronger with each passing day, and a more noticeable transformation was under way. Trust for myself and others was slowly being restored. I refrained from new relationships and focused on repairing the old ones.

Fear, guilt, and shame began to loosen their grip. Their hold on me was weakened as my relationship with God was strengthened. I was in a process, but I continued to battle with my excessive drinking. In fact, it took a turn for the worse. I spent change that I had laying around the house to buy liquor. Sometimes I walked and sometimes I took a cab. There were even times when I walked home at night from the liquor store if I didn't have enough for both a bottle and a taxi.

I started attending church again; this time, a little more than once a month. I found the courage to return to the church I grew up attending. I managed not to drink on Saturday evenings so that I was sober on Sunday morning. That in itself was progress.

Slowly, I began to let God back in. There was also something else going on, and I didn't know exactly why it was happening. I couldn't sleep. Almost every morning, I woke up around 3am and could not go back to sleep. When I told my mother about it, she told me to learn the 23rd Psalm. I recited it nightly; not realizing how the power of that psalm had an impact on my life. God always loved me, and I started telling myself a new story. What better way than to begin by declaring, *"The Lord is my Shepherd, I have all that I need."* God loved me and He became my strength. Truly, I lacked nothing with Him.

***

In Him is where we find rest from the storms and challenges of life. In His word, He promises peace and to calm our worries, fears, and woes. A renewed life and strength to move on and face hardships because He is always with us are more of His assurances. He is the light in darkness and has a purpose for our lives that will bring honor to His name. FATHER KNOWS BEST, and we can't continue to venture down the road of disobedience. He says that He will chasten those He loves. When we submit to His will rather than trying to go it on our own, He will then begin to lift us up. He has set us apart and wants to bless us abundantly.

Although I set the pen aside, a new chapter was being written. I found the security I was looking for on my new journey though I felt very alone. The damage on the inside was still there, and I found some relief because, once again, my secrets were safe and remained tucked away. This really only meant that they were not yet resolved. Most of them were never even revealed until I wrote this story. Here, right here in this book is where the process of healing began.

By far, thus far, this has not been an easy challenge. The Lord doesn't push Himself on us but longs for us, His children, to come back home. He desires a relationship with us. He nudged me and then removed the distractions so I could hear Him softly call and say, "Daughter, this is the way. Walk in it."

On My Way

Christmas was still my favorite time of year, and what I loved so much about it seemed to be renewed. My mom asked me what I wanted for Christmas that year, and I pronounced proudly, *"A bible."* She seemed a little surprised at my response, but Christmas morning, amongst all of the other wonderful gifts I received, there was the very thing I asked for – a bible with a women's devotional book, and I was excited!

I had an opportunity to be reconnected with my first boyfriend, David. At first, I thought, *Perfect,* but I vowed to refrain from jumping into relationships. Besides, I was still drinking. So, I sought God this time regarding the matter. Ultimately, I prayed and told God that I didn't want anyone or anything that would serve as a distraction to me learning more about Him and myself. I was starting to learn how to stand on my own without feigned love and alcohol. Slowly but surely, I was moving away from that life, and I trusted that if David and I were meant to be, He would bring him back under different circumstances.

***

You know, when we boldly ask for something, we often think we'll get just what we asked for, but when the response manifests totally different than what we expected, we can't go back on our word.

***

The more I talked with God, the more things began to fall away. I knew how to talk to Him, but I wanted to know and understand what was written in His word. I also wanted to learn how to listen to Him and recognize when He was speaking. It wasn't yet clear to me that He was very much present through everything that occurred. As I looked back at those dangerous situations that could have proven fatal and saw others reuniting with old loves and overcoming circumstances that came along with those relationships, I wondered why that couldn't happen for me. Deep down inside, I already knew the answer – *that* life was truly over, and He removed the distractions.

After I returned to church, Sis. Faith told me that her son was returning to pastor the church and he was very good. Before she could finish her thought, I asked defensively, *"Good at what?"* I think she saw that I was somewhat disconnected and needed help. I was finally able to share with her about my ex, Leo, and his unauthorized intrusion into my home. Maybe it better explained why I was so defensive. I allowed people in slowly in certain areas of my life, while others still remained off limits. I was told that I behaved like someone who had been victimized. All this time, I thought I was hiding, but my actions demonstrated the contrary.

Besides, I was doing well on my own. I had it figured out. What I didn't need was anyone poking around, trying to fix me, when they didn't know me. For me, the pastor wasn't any more than someone I came to listen to on Sunday, and even then, I had little expectation of learning much from him. Pastors didn't care if you showed up on a regular basis. I never witnessed one pastor who went to look for a member who was not in attendance. Why go after the one that got away if you have the majority who still came?

***

What happens when you go to a place in search of something and no one points you in the right direction? I know there are some who would say, "Leave and never look back." I think it's okay to look momentarily, just long enough to see how far God brought you. He will then begin to position people around you, who will confirm His word in you.

***

Toward the end of each service, when they extended the invitation to discipleship and announced that the doors of the church were opened, that was my cue to leave. For some reason, this time was different; the invitation seemed personal. I was nervous, almost as if someone was looking directly at me. This time, I really waited for the doors to be opened. It was under the leadership of the new pastor, Dr. Wheeler, that this occurred. He was now the pastor of the church we both grew up attending. He knew who my parents were but knew very little about me personally.

God knew just how much of a skeptic I was, and like Gideon, the reluctant warrior in the book of Judges, I too asked for a series of confirmations. Well, the pastor delivered a sermon that Sunday morning that was not easy to shake. After service, I spoke to him and then headed straight out to the liquor store before it closed. With every visit, I felt more uneasy– as if I was being watched. I bought a bottle and took the quickest route home. I locked the door behind me and thought I was safe from piercing gazes. My conscience was letting me know that it was wrong, and finally, I asked God for help to break the hold that alcohol had over me. I knew it wasn't going to be an easy task, but slowly, I became strong enough to break free.

I continued attending church services, and after hearing a few more messages, my curiosity was sparked to learn more about the stories in the bible. I read and re-read the same stories over and over and studied some of the words as they appeared in different bible translations. I performed character studies, only to learn that there was truth and wisdom in every story I read.

As a result, I had even more questions. I learned more about our Father and took home the notes I wrote down. I was intrigued by the stories that sounded like they were written with me in mind! I became very much interested in hearing more about God's *unlikely sources*, as I like to call them. It was through their stories that I discovered hope and learned about faith, forgiveness, and healing.

CHAPTER FOUR
DESPERATE

Mark 5:25-26 *"And a certain woman, which had an issue of blood twelve years, And had suffered many things of many physicians, and had spent all that she had, and was nothing bettered, but rather grew worse."*

In scripture, she was known as the woman with an issue. Her name was never mentioned, but her story reads as if we've known her all our lives. As we journey through life, we too can quite easily become known for our issues – *That's the girl who had a baby out of wedlock. That's the boy who was locked up for robbing the corner store.* Personally, I better understand how she became the woman with the issue of blood. Indeed, she suffered a great deal even while under the care of many doctors and after she spent all she had.[2]

This nameless woman cried out to be healed and sought after everyone and everything in her quest, yet all she found failed to save her. Although the story only shares that the woman had an issue of blood, like her, we really don't entirely know what anyone may be dealing with. Perhaps, like many of us, she even pursued temporary fixes and sought comfort or relief in drugs, alcohol, sex, and other seemingly gratifying activities. What's certain is that all her efforts were futile and only worsened the matter. It wasn't until the woman encountered Jesus that she was healed of her infirmities and loosed from what held her bound all those years.

***

---
[2] Mark 5:26 paraphrased

I called out to everyone, but no one could help. I looked for safety that no one was able to provide. Love from people – flawed and limited; love from God – perfect and everlasting.

This particular narrative had such an impact on me. When I heard it, it pierced my heart and pricked my soul. No matter how much I pretended, I identified with the woman and her issues.

***

After I heard about the woman with the issue of blood during a Sunday morning service, I couldn't wait to get home. She too sought answers, maybe even validation, but in her own effort, found no permanent solution to her condition. After I entered my apartment and closed the door behind me, I fell to my knees and cried out, *"God, I can't do this any longer. I can't carry all of this on my own. You are God and bigger than my alcohol addiction and desires."* Desires – the greatest one was to be loved, but what I called love displayed no true interest in my well-being.

I petitioned Him to destroy the strongholds and loose me from my infirmities like He did for the woman with the issue of blood. I needed to be delivered from the wounded little girl inside, who held on to anger and gained strength because I fed my frailties. The victimized child threw tantrums when things didn't go her way or if the world she created to protect herself was disrupted. She had to let go and grow up, and I had to let go and let God, else the underdeveloped little girl in me would hinder my ability to move forward. Our inner selves grow according to how they are fed. The recipe of lies left me stagnated and stuck in a cycle of reliving the pain of the past. It also kept at arm's length those who truly loved and cared for me.

Time and again, I refused to seek help, but as the weight became most unbearable, I saw the affects it had on my children. I really didn't want them to suffer for my sin and wrongdoing. I was tired of landing in the same places, but I had to change the source of what I thought could save me, and I finally grew desperate for the One who could.

The relationships I pursued only made additional contributions to pain and suffering for my family and me. I grew exhausted of the temporary fixes that offered no relief, and one of the consequences was the toll it took on the relationship with my children. I transitioned from drinking the "hard stuff" to drinking wine and lots of it, and it fueled frequent arguments between my son and me. My daughter wasn't excluded. One evening after I threw myself on the floor, my daughter started distancing herself from me and became more of an introvert. She hardly spoke anymore. My drinking made her sad and it kept us apart. I did my best to hide it from her, but she always knew when I was drinking. When she suspected, she sniffed up close even when I tried to cover up with chewing gum or by brushing my teeth. Even though I was their mother and a grownup, it did not justify my actions that resulted in their hurt. I knew I needed to stop. The very ones I vowed to protect from everyone else needed protection from me. I was determined to flip the script on how I was living my life. I had to fight those demons that lived on the inside, and it was time to issue a notice of eviction. A new determination to live the life and become the woman God destined me to be required it.

I realized that all of the previous alarms and warnings were promptings from the Holy Spirit who attempted to lead me away from danger and preserve my connection to the Father. My parents and my children were proud of my decision to make changes. I felt so much guilt for what I put them through. The most difficult feat was learning to forgive myself.

***

One day on my way to work, I stopped at the bodega on the corner. One of the owners who knew Leo and me asked, *"Are you still with that guy?"*

I responded, *"No, I'm no longer with him."*

He said, *"Good Mija, that guy was loco."*

I ran into other acquaintances who also inquired about that relationship, and many shared the same sentiment. Some even went as far as to thank God when they found out that we were no longer together. Those brief conversations in passing left me amazed at how many people were concerned, even the nurse in the doctor's office who asked probing questions because she suspected that I was a victim of abuse. One day, I went into the office for a routine visit, and the assistant got upset because I had a bruise on my leg. I thought she overreacted. I didn't even remember how the bruise got there. If I told them I fell, they would think that was an obvious cover story. Ultimately, it became clearer just how many others perceived the threat and how God's grace, the prayers of others, and my willingness to change brought me out of that situation.

I pray for the day that abuse will no longer remain silent and those victimized by it won't feel guilty or ashamed. Oftentimes, abusers were also abused, and both are victims in need of healing.

***

The most obvious revelation derived from the nameless woman with the issue of blood sent me running back to church every Sunday morning. Her story became my personal testimony, and little did I know that God would use my story to testify to others that He is indeed bigger than all our issues.

The nameless woman in the story found no comfort in the places she passed through, nor did she find anyone who could heal her. All of that changed when she heard about a man named Jesus, who came to heal the sick and bind up the brokenhearted. Her faith fueled her hope that if she could just touch the hem of His garment, she would indeed be made whole. When she touched Him, immediately the flow of blood ceased, and she knew that she was cured of her afflictions.

When we turn away from those things that only give us momentary satisfaction and turn to Jesus for a permanent solution; we will receive our healing and be set free from what ails us.

At once, Jesus realized that power had left Him. He turned around in the crowd and asked, *"Who touched Me?"* [3] There were many that followed, but one person's faith stood out. Jesus asked to see if she would be a witness and testify of Him. The woman came and fell down before Him in humble submission. Vulnerable and transparent, she openly came forward. She was not the least bit worried about the crowd or what others thought.

Jesus responded, *"Daughter, your faith has made you well. Go in peace."*

The woman with her issues was made free from the warfare, trials, and chaos that governed over her life for twelve long years. Out of her own desperation, she realized she couldn't be like everyone else in the crowd. She had to reposition herself and press her way through. This woman grew tired of her situation and the way she was living. Her story showed me that there comes a time when we must come out from the crowd, humble ourselves, and look up to Him. We have to silence the outside noises and other people's voices and bend our knees, even crawl or stretch out, until we touch Him like a baby determined to get to their destination.

***

The woman, whose name wasn't as important as her story or her demonstration of faith and determination, postured herself and apprehended her breakthrough. God determined that she had had enough. He speaks to us in a still small voice. If we quiet ourselves, we will hear Him declare the same for us, "Enough," calling fullness to our void and empty places and commanding order out of all the chaos. God will cause what is watering our infirmities and abetting

---

[3] Mark 5:31-34

our losses to dry up, and anything that is unlike Him will begin to fall away. Her faith was the precursor to her breakthrough and was displayed in the pressing through that positioned her to receive her gracious and glorious outcome.

We have to come to Jesus with a made-up mind, determined to be healed and set free, and ready to witness to others about what the Lord has done. I am not saying we must write a "tell all," but we can share our struggles with others who may be going through similar situations. No, it's not easy; it wasn't meant to be. We all come with our own set of challenges, but we are never alone. There are other people who traveled down similar roads, and their triumphs lend hope so we will know that it is possible to obtain freedom. The pain and suffering will subside although the scars remain. They are the reminders of how something beautiful and unique was birthed through our pain. We were meant to change lives with the message of how we overcame.

Many of us have made mistakes, and our circumstances influenced what we believed about ourselves. We felt unworthy of anything better and found it difficult to return home. Because of our limitations in love and trust, we placed those same limitations on a limitless God, which made it difficult for us to see that God wants everything to do with us and waits for us with open arms.

I admired the woman for her fearless courage to push past her troubles and beyond those who probably viewed her as unworthy. Reliance on wisdom, knowledge, and understanding of who He is and who He is in us will see us through every situation. He has already provided what we need to break through. I love to read the story of the woman with the issue of blood. I personalized it, as if Jesus had me in mind when it occurred. I imagined what this woman must have gone through after suffering for so long.

During biblical times, this same woman probably never thought that Jesus would use her to witness; the same holds true today. Many people believe that God won't use them because of their past. We must learn to be careful of what we believe about ourselves and remain mindful of words we accept that don't align with what God has already said about us.

The contents of the next chapter are entirely up to us. The journey is never easy, and we all are presented with a choice – either we will let go and allow God to pen His account, or we'll close the book – end of story. We have no right to deprive others of our light.

Sometimes, we have to put on our best even when we feel our worst and press our way. Even if the way is watered with our tears, the stirrings of our hearts speak directly to the Father, and the heart is what He wants devoted to Him. Our best outward appearance, though important, may not be the primary focus when in pursuit of freedom from our infirmities.

Think again on the woman with the issue of blood, who pressed her way to get to Jesus. Her outward presentation was not even mentioned; in fact, I venture to say that it might have been least important in comparison to her desperation for her breakthrough. A mind undergoing transformation and a repentant heart is the course that leads directly to Christ.

CHAPTER FIVE
RELEASE THE HOSTAGES!

Emotional hostage situations are often formed in co-dependent relationships. They are established through the unspoken and, most often, unrealistic expectations placed upon others who are held accountable unawares for our emotional well-being or distress. This type of scenario burdens both the hostage as well as the hostage-taker and hinders both parties from behavior that supports healthy bonds and relational interactions. A vital aspect of the healing process requires the release of people held hostage by our emotions.

***

I had difficultly chronicling significant improvements in my walk, and it became obvious that there were pending struggles thwarting my advancement. Finally, I asked myself, *"What are you really doing, Kimberly?"*

This personal assessment revealed emerging bouts of rage that constantly led to negative altercations and poor outcomes when dealing with others. The goal of this self-inventory was to determine the reason why my progress and positive strides weren't yielding more considerable outcomes.

I functioned diligently around the problem in an unconscious effort not to address the problem. I worked faithfully in the church. I told others about the love of God and spoke words of encouragement to incite health, help, and healing. So, what was the problem? Why was it so easy to help others and overlook my own need? Why didn't the same words of encouragement have the same effect on me? No matter how much I served, read, and studied, the broken *"child"* remained on the inside and waited for her turn to receive the help she so desperately needed. Of course, there were many to blame for her pain, but someone had to be held responsible to heal her, right? Wrong – I was very wrong; hence, my discovery.

I WAS A CERTIFIED HOSTAGE-TAKER and guilty of placing impractical expectations on others. This was a difficult revelation and something I wasn't proud of or wanted readily to admit. I believe it began that night long ago when I stood in front of the mirror and the words echoed from within, *"It's your fault."*

Undoubtedly, the unlawful incident that preceded that instant was demoralizing. No one had a right to violate another person, and it should have never happened. However, at the moment of that harrowing accusation, the need to defend myself against it rendered me incapable of my own accountability. Instead, I manipulated blame in order to authenticate my own emotional injury.

I blamed God, my Father. I alienated my parents, who had absolutely nothing to do with that particular situation but were indicted because, somehow, the past incident with my cousin, Derrick, became relevant. I concealed the matter from my friends, isolated them and covertly held them responsible for my pain. My exes were substitutions, who should have provided the love I needed to remove the guilt and shame, along with a host of others who survived the brunt of the abuse wreaked upon them from my emotional wounds. It was only by the grace of God that their love survived my pain.

Those words, *"It's your fault,"* repeatedly rehearsed became a cement-like layer over the scars and impeded the much-needed process of healing. The same energy I invested to wreak havoc in the lives of my hostages was the same effort needed to negotiate on behalf of my faith to jumpstart my recovery and manifest good from all the hurt and pain endured.

Over time, the voice of condemnation faded and was replaced by the still small voice of the Holy Spirit, who spoke constructive conviction. *"If only you will stop allowing pride and stubbornness to hinder you from the necessary internal work that needs to be done, then you will be more receptive to the truth when it's presented to you,"* were the words that pierced my heart.

He also admonished me of jealousy and how it was a knee-jerk reaction to the need to be justified and validated. I knew I had to go deeper and do the work. To be loosed from the ungodly strongholds that held me hostage, the first step was to stop placing blame on others as a method for avoiding the truth and justification for not looking more closely at myself. I had to fully trust God with my wounds from the past and sort through the residue that triggered old feelings of bitterness and rage.

The truth is that God never left me during the storms I endured, but rage, bitterness, stubbornness, and pride built a wall and barricaded Him outside the places where I needed Him. God intended for us to rise above our circumstances, soar to places in Him, and live life abundantly as foretold. The greatest difficulty for me was letting go.

Trust and forgiveness are fundamental components of the healing process. Forgiveness is more about us than it is about anyone else. Besides, we cannot be forgiven unless we forgive. Unless we trust God and forgive those who hurt us, we give place and power to pain by reliving past instances. Was I blaming God? Yes, and I had to come clean. I was angry about all that happened to me and didn't know how to trust Him again with my heart.

God knows everything about us and is already aware of any charge we hold against Him. It is imperative to repair our relationship with Him before we can hope or expect to have wholesome relationships with others.

CHAPTER SIX
UNFINISHED BUSINESS

Pride ruling in our hearts narrates to us that we don't need help from anyone and that we can do it on our own, but when truth speaks and draws attention to the repeated cycles that impede our progress, sure indicators of unfinished business and unresolved issues are uncovered.

My cousin, Derrick, who crept into my room that night, was the first to violate my trust and his actions initiated a cycle of confusion. Years later, I received word that he'd been hurt, and what became obvious was the emptiness I had on the inside – no emotion, no sadness, no tears, not even an ounce of concern toward his welfare. I was startled by my response. Was I that harsh? That's when I knew something was very wrong. My heart started to become like one made of stone, and that was not my desired outcome. A new heart was needed; and I wanted God to transplant the old for one that was tender toward him and others.

My relationship with my father was also collateral damage because I held him responsible for not defending my honor, when he wasn't even aware of the incident with Derrick. I was embarrassed because he didn't send Derrick packing, but the more simple answer was to talk to him or tell him what happened. Instead, this became another justification that I was the victim and needed to protect myself from even the potential of being hurt again.

One day, I spoke with my mentor while she prepared her study lesson plan for the week. She shared the title, "Unfinished Business," and right away, I knew how the topic was relevant to me. Before long, I disclosed my life experiences into her confidence. She evaluated that I conducted myself like a person who was hiding abuse and coddling the memories. I was surprised at her discovery since I became such a pro at disguising my injuries. She continued and finally asked, *"Have you ever talked to anyone about this, Kimberly?"*

I could not form the words to respond; instead, tears fell from my eyes that indicated that the answer was no. Actually, that was the first time I ever told anyone. I relived the abuse daily, mentally, and emotionally and actually empowered the pain by nurturing my wounds through victimhood.

I learned that it was acceptable and even expected to admit that it still hurt, and, more importantly, I needed to be honest about what was going on with me. A new and unfamiliar process ensued –first, acknowledgment; and then release according to the scriptures, *"Casting all your care upon Him, for He cares for you."* [4] Once I made the decision to turn them over to the Father, I was responsible to leave them in His capable hands and trust Him with the outcome. Great intention and a strong prayer life were necessary to persevere until those areas were healed.

***

The enemy exerts power over us through strongholds. Strongholds are formed through fear, anger, depression, abuse, abandonment, rejection, low or no self-worth, and self-loathing. Seeds planted and watered produce weeds of bitterness, worthlessness, doubt, guilt, shame, and rage and choke the life out of the beauty hidden within.

Over the years, my list became extensive. I even harbored very strong feelings against my cousin's mother because she was responsible for him being born. Although it sounded absurd, the mental and emotional strongholds built a platform for those types of thoughts. Because I embraced the victim mentality, I always sought and expected to be

---

[4] 1 Peter 5:7 NKJV

wounded, my inability to forgive became corrosive, and I became paralyzed in spite of all my efforts.

***

We must be willing to venture beyond surface feelings and examine the behaviors we exhibit during interactions with others. The purpose of such an activity is to arrive at the root cause of the affliction. As difficult as it may be, the discovery then allows for the process of acknowledgment that leads to release. Otherwise, the never-ending cycle of unfinished business continues to repeat itself.

The ultimate intention is to root out and destroy ungodly strongholds. When God reveals strongholds or besetting sin in our lives, we must humble ourselves, confess our transgressions. break agreement with that behavior, and work to remove the root cause of the sin that led to that stronghold. Learning the truth of the word of God and making a commitment to live out His word in our daily lives helps us to wage war against the contrary thoughts that will try and creep back in. We are instructed to take every thought captive until it becomes obedient to that of Christ.[5]

It's time to release those we charged and deemed responsible, whether by verbal or mental admission. If we don't deal with our unfinished business, it will surely deal with us.

***

I had no idea how big a part pride played in my inability to move on. Pride even kept me from admitting that I was in pride. As a result, a huge part of my unfinished business was to release those I held hostage because I came to the conclusion that they contributed to my pain. Years of resentment shackled them to the stories I replayed in my mind. *"If it wasn't for them..."* was the introduction to every narrative. It never dawned on me that those thoughts did nearly as much damage as what actually happened to me.

[5] 2Corinthians 10:4-5 paraphrased

My uncle sent me two throwback pictures of me when I was much younger. One was of me in my christening dress with my mom, and the other was with my dad who was showing me something. What I remembered wasn't the content little girl in the photos but the one who endured events that instigated a desperate, validation-seeking journey.

I spent so much time with the hurt and angry version of myself that the girl of yesteryear, who like clockwork knew when her parents would come home and benefitted from their attention to her needs, was lost.

Those moments captured on camera awoke a determination to do the internal work. Again, I reached for my notebook and pen and wrote a declaration of truth and commitment.

***

This day, I, Kimberly Mitchell, release everyone upon whom I placed unrealistic charges and expectations. In doing so, I know that I am not only releasing them, but myself. God, please cleanse me of any leftover residue and heal the places and wounds in my heart. I am releasing them and choosing to forgive so that I can truly experience God's love and forgiveness. I know that it is only then that I can move from victim to victor. God, please remove what has kept me bound and has hindered the natural flow between You and me. In the name of Jesus; Amen!

After the prayer, I named each person and what I held against them.

This was my personal exercise, and, obviously, you can add or take away to suit your specific situation. This declaration is not something you have to share with anyone else. Keep it for your own personal record as a reminder of the vow you made to the Father. The most important task is to make a binding agreement between you and God. I implore you not to go another day bound by strongholds that keep you from God's blessings.

***

In order to function at our absolute best and get on with what's ahead of us, we must be willing to resolve unfinished business. We must endure being inconvenienced while we discover our true identity and are molded into who we were meant to become so that He can display the new and incredible as outlined in 2Corinthians 5:17, *"Therefore if any man be in Christ, he is a new creature: old things are passed away; behold, all things are become new."*

CHAPTER SEVEN
BAPTISM SUNDAY

Romans 6:4 *"Therefore we were buried with Him by baptism into death, in order that just as Christ was raised from the dead by the glory of the Father, so we too may walk in a new way of life."* (HCSB)

After 27 years of what seemed like torment and a relentless battle, the situation with my dad came to a head when, during a heated argument, I blurted out that he never cared. I discovered that he knew absolutely nothing about the incident with Derrick. That realization nearly drove me back to guilt and shame, and I immediately thought about all the time that could have been spared if I had only spoken up sooner. Had he known, my father would have protected me, and I could have avoided a lot of the pain endured by going it alone.

I spoke forth the lie that fueled the resentment toward my father; the lie the enemy fed me over the years compiled with every incident that contributed additional injury.

I was growing stronger spiritually, mentally, and physically, and it was time to wash away the soot of my past. The plot against my life became clearer and how the enemy used the incident with my cousin to get me off track, hoping that the seed of abuse would continue to manifest through alcohol, broken relationships, and misuse by self and others. The goal was to sidetrack me enough to derail me from the demonstration of God's purpose through my life. Adversely, his attempts only drew me closer to my heavenly Father and my earthly dad as well. Our restored relationship far exceeded the one that was lost and also became an integral part of the next leg of my journey.

***

I was given an opportunity to be baptized a second time. On Sunday, September 28, 2014, I was baptized at the same church where my first baptism took place. This second chance, as I perceived it, was just as important as the first and came at a pivotal time in my life. There were quite a few others who started anew that day. Although our paths were unique, we were all on the same journey toward victory in Jesus Christ, our Savior.

Being baptized a second time wasn't about a do-over. The choice to do so was multifaceted. I was tired of running into dead ends. I was tired of hurting. I was tired of looking and expecting to be saved by those who also needed saving. Self-discovery was an integral contributor to the decisions that led me to such an important conclusion. The obstacles and former hindrances needed to be removed, and I wanted to be relieved of the weight of the heavy burdens.

When I put on the baptismal robe, I noticed that it was quite roomy. My attention was drawn to the length and how it draped over my feet onto the floor. I imagined the full magnitude of my Father's covering and knew it was a perfect fit. It was time; time to wash away the stains of the old that could not accompany me into the place of newness. Besides, they no longer fit into God's purpose for my life. It was indeed a "perfect" day. There weren't enough words to describe how beautiful it was. The sun seemed to shine just a little brighter, and the water temperature in the baptismal pool was just right.

I sat next to my father as we watched a baby who played affectionately during her dedication. I wondered what my dad was thinking when he smiled as we looked on. I imagined my parents standing there while the pastor sprinkled water on my head. They were devoted, and, even as a young child, dedicated me back to the Lord as a student in Christ. Just as an infant grows and matures into adulthood, the example of their faith was the investment toward my decision to walk in the ways of Christ.

Water baptism is a seal, an outward sign that displays an inward decision to become a part of God's family; and evidence that old things are passed away as we become one with Christ. It's a commitment toward a different life – a new life. We don't immediately become perfect but pledge to strive daily to become more like Him.

Our bodies are temples, dwelling places for the Holy Spirit. He's our counselor and help in times of trouble. The Holy Spirit convicts us of wrong thinking that leads to wrongdoing and advises us away from places and situations that we should avoid. No matter what we face, we should always be intentional about turning away from things that are displeasing to God. We must study the word of God, be obedient to what it says, and remain accountable for our own actions and how we treat others. We must maintain our faith and trust in the Lord. That's the way to walk with Him.

That day, I made a bold statement to everyone who attended as witnesses as well as a private decision to allow God to heal every part of my life and reveal the hidden things even unbeknownst to me. I took the first step toward the courageous feat of coming face to face with myself in light of Him. I knew that He never left or abandoned me and that He would guide me through the darkest valley and lead me to the plush places; and it was all possible because He was always with me.[6]

---

[6] Psalm 23:4 paraphrased

CHAPTER EIGHT
PIECES OF THE PUZZLE

Philippians 1:6 *"Being confident of this very thing, that he which hath begun a good work in you will perform it until the day of Jesus Christ:"*

Puzzles, in my opinion, were the worst things ever invented. The outside of the box displayed a picturesque scene that was often very inspiring. The idea of achieving that particular outcome provided a great deal of excitement, until you opened the box, only to discover just how tedious and meticulous of an exercise you were in for. What was supposed to be fun and exciting instigated bouts of frustration, and the enticing cover photo turned into a mess of seemingly random pieces whose assembly required a lot more effort than anticipated.

As a mother, I dreaded the thought of my children receiving puzzles as gifts. I proposed almost any other item on the toy store shelf other than puzzles, yet somehow they were still drawn to them in spite of my unusual dislike for them.

Even when I worked in a classroom full of five-year-old young children, who were just starting out, I carefully redirected their curious minds to find other sources of enjoyment that were more immediately gratifying and a lot less complicated. Unknowingly, I imposed my issues onto them and indirectly taught them the art of self-defeat before they even learned how to tie their shoes without assistance from adults.

How would they ever learn patience and endurance involved in process? I believe that was one of the lessons embedded in the activity of assembling puzzles. Perhaps if I accepted similar challenges earlier on, I would have been more disciplined and patient throughout the stages of my own life.

Like checkers and chess, puzzles require some element of strategy. Tactical and accurate placement of the pieces is the way to arrive at the beautiful picture on the box that prompted dauntless engagement in the first place. The same is conveyed by the ordering of the fragments of our lives, purposed to tell a story. If any of the parts are omitted, the story is altered and incomplete; and if any of the parts are out of place, then the story is distorted.

Investments of time, patience, tenacity, and encouragement are key components to this assembly process. Eventually, the sum of the parts will reveal the bigger picture. I wonder if the person who invented puzzles figured that out. Perhaps they were given divine vision to pair puzzles with the process of our lives that result in the image impressed in our minds before we opened the box.

***

Alopecia

The greatest challenge in my life was finding out how the pieces fit together. Aside from everything that had already taken place, I was confronted with how to come to terms with alopecia. I asked God, *"Why me?"* I really couldn't understand why losing my hair was required. I was left with feelings of inadequacy and wondered if God really loved me. The answer to that question was most unexpected. I needed to see the beauty in myself first and develop compassion for others who also felt inadequate.

Alopecia is an autoimmune disease often associated with stress. Doctors have researched and still haven't figured out why or how the system's response to stress is to attack the hair follicles. *How about, I was stressed about losing my hair?* Alopecia is not an easy dilemma. A woman with no hair is almost inconceivable and a stigma of sorts. Some embrace not having hair, while others feel ashamed and very self-conscious.

After a brief study break one day, I decided to take a few selfies. For the first time, I took a picture without wearing a wig. I raised the camera and looked up. As I smiled, tears fell from my eyes, and, in that moment, I knew I was prepared to present myself, as is – no filter, no wig.

I decided to carry out that decision on the day of my second baptism and was pleasantly surprised at the feedback I received. Sisters were very encouraging, and I believe my courage awakened something in them. That's when I realized the dual purpose of my unfortunate situation worked on my behalf as well as theirs.

Understandably, alopecia can contribute to lack of self-esteem. The only person outside of my immediate family who knew that I suffered from it was Leo, aka Mr. Perfect. He was probably the reason I ignored the signs in the first place. He made me feel beautiful despite what I was going through. Our breakup forced me to come to terms with what was *really* going on inside without a buffer. As long as Leo stood between reality and me, I would not have been able to respond to the opportunities that awaited or walk through the doors that were about to open.

***

While I worked as a secretary at one of the local schools, a teacher and her teen daughter hosted a fundraiser for children who suffered from hair loss. I spoke with the mother and wasn't ashamed to share my experience for the first time. Her eyes filled with tears while I recounted the details.

She asked if I would talk with her daughter. It was obvious they both endured a great deal of pain over their ordeal, but neither of them was to blame. Her daughter and I had a private conversation, and, with some embarrassment, she admitted that her anger over the situation caused her to question God. Ironically, it was He who caused our paths to converge at that designated place and at that particular time. In that instant, we all received what we needed from God. My eyes were filled with tears, and it became abundantly clear that another puzzle piece had found its place.

Alcoholism

Excessive drinking is quite often a camouflage for more deep-seated matters. For me, it was a temporary painkiller and a hideaway from the issues that aroused that pain. My struggle with alcohol and the process of my rehabilitation deposited a great degree of wisdom through the lessons learned as a result.

Someone asked how I defeated alcoholism. I believe that the inquiry was prompted by that person's struggle, so I cited my firsthand knowledge in response. I told them that defeat was a process that began with a decision and commitment to persevere until breakthrough. I spoke openly and honestly about how the temptation remained like a thorn in my side – a constant reminder of the need for strength and support from our heavenly Father. I encouraged an adamant prayer life and down-right refusal to quit.

I also advised new activities to fill up the time previously occupied by drinking. I traded my need for a drink with my love and passion for writing. Pen in hand and armed with my notebook, I became lost in the world of words that flowed from my heart and escaped through the pen, and, ultimately, another puzzle piece found its place.

Toastmasters

My inspiration to encourage and motivate others through speaking sent me on a slightly different journey. I tried the short route via attendance of a few multi-level marketing venues, but I was met with the challenge of condensing the sales pitch. I over-talked the product and could never stick to the script provided. Multi-level marketing wasn't for everyone and proved to be an inadequate fit for me.

While I searched for a more comparable outlet, I discovered Toastmasters. The format of this group taught me to better express myself verbally and built up confidence and courage to speak about events in my life. I still found it frighteningly difficult to talk about molestation and rape. Hearing the truth from my own voice was like removing a band-aid that was stuck to a wound and demolishing the walls within that provided convenient hiding places.

Not only did I learn to speak in less than eight minutes, I discovered key leadership skills and additional components of my authentic identity. After every speech, the listeners were encouraged but constructively pointed out that I was still holding back. There was an exercise called "Ice Breaker" where I had to select a topic and compose a brief story about how and why I ended up at Toastmasters. I created a series on faith and purpose and hinted around the talking points that made me uncomfortable.

Some time later, I was asked to give a speech at a club contest. I thought I was ready until the interviewer asked how I recovered from being molested. It was plainly obvious that I still carted around the pain associated with that area in my life. Talking about it was very different than writing about it, and I knew then that the speaking element was going to take a bit of getting used to. As a result, however, I became even more determined to prevail in that area. While the picture of who I was becoming became clearer, the pieces of the puzzle this phase provided were also better aligned.

***

Puzzles, in their own right, weren't bad at all. Pieces put in their proper places revealed more of the hidden outcome. Change was what was occurring, and the once blank canvas now gave way to a more precise portrait of who I was becoming. I no longer needed outside approval, validation, or permission to be me. Everything that happened and the people associated with those instances were instruments in my discovery process. I was now responsible for aligning my thoughts with how those pieces contributed to my personal growth and development.

A completed puzzle is actually a narrative; a story that someone even not yet born may be privileged to read. The stories become the tools for their encouragement when they open the box of their own lives and need to arrange the mess of pieces displayed. Our image on the cover is a snapshot of hope for those sorting through the same struggles and afflictions; and our tactical approaches to assembling the puzzles become valuable lesson segments meant to be shared with others.

***

CHAPTER NINE
EXCUSE ME WHILE I CHANGE

2 Corinthians 3:16-18 *"But whenever someone turns to the Lord, the veil is taken away. For the Lord is the Spirit, and wherever the Spirit of the Lord is, there is freedom. So all of us who have had that veil removed can see and reflect the glory of the Lord. And the Lord–who is the Spirit–makes us more and more like him as we are changed into his glorious image."* (NLT)

Everything created by God has a specific and predetermined purpose in the earth, even bugs. Yuck! Yes, the hand of our Creator designed them with purpose in mind. A wise person once advised me to pay closer attention to the things I found repulsive. I decided to take notice of what we easily discard or deem insignificant and explore the intention behind them. Pushing past how we feel and doing what is required is a catalyst for growth, change, and maturity.

Look at the butterfly, for example. The beginning stages aren't nearly as appealing as the end result. What begins as a caterpillar must endure a death of sorts in order to be transformed into a butterfly. The lowest and longest stage of the process is the cocoon phase, but at the time of change, two distinct things happen: (1) a name change – what was once referred to as a caterpillar becomes known as a butterfly; and (2) a physical change – the emergence of a new creature with brilliant and colorful wings.

Walking in the ways of Christ is life-changing, and to live the free and abundant life He promised, we must first be willing to die to ourselves and devote our lives to Him. Even the not-so-pleasant and shameful things are a part of our process of change. God wants to take us from our low places and grow and elevate us in Him. Much like the butterfly, we too must endure what is often painful and mundane but absolutely necessary to equip us and ultimately transform us into His beautiful, new creations. God, who declared the end from the beginning, has been at work in us to bring about fulfillment of our divine destinies. He has every intention to cultivate and nurture the seed He planted, and nothing concerning us is lost with Him.

The narrative implied by the development of a butterfly was carefully penned by the hand of our Creator and carries a message that reminds us to look beyond our present circumstance and believe for the outcome. The story presents a lovely account of how even the low and dark places contribute to our divine transformation.

***

"If our circumstances don't change; perhaps they were meant to change us."

Stages of development prepare us for what lies ahead. Substantial growth and maturity are prerequisite criteria before we can advance to where God is ultimately leading us. Many have the misconception that once we surrender our lives to Christ, all the former things immediately fall away. This mindset gives place to the enemy of our souls and convinces us that salvation is all that is required; when actually, the journey to transformation has just begun. We have to work out our salvation, stay committed to the process, and endure till the end. Instead of expecting God to just remove or change our issues, situations, and circumstances, we have to learn that He often uses them as instruments of refinement in our change process. Challenges develop our faith and make us stronger, while the storms of life build up endurance.

***

My stubborn nature and tendency toward conflict was impeding my spiritual growth and character development. It was high time that I faced those shortcomings and assumed responsibility for my actions. It wasn't realistic to ask God to remove conflicts altogether but to teach me how to conduct myself in a godly manner in the face of adverse challenges. Ironically, the same issues I wanted to eliminate, He used as agents of change. He took my strong will and stubbornness and transformed them into passion and fortitude to withstand until the evidence of change manifested in my life.

Other issues evolved as well. One was my desire to feel loved, but I wasn't able to identify or receive it because of complications with trust. Settling for lust only satisfied the temporary desires of the flesh and blinded me to what real love offered. I knew there was more and that those cases weren't the totality of my existence. I wasn't giving up until I arrived at the place called change, and I made no apology for my determination.

Then there was my addiction to alcohol, which birthed my diligence in faith. My dependency on the substance wasn't formed overnight but became habitual over time, so time was also a factor in my overcoming. When I discovered that I had to participate in my deliverance, I reformed my prayers and asked for the strength to lay it down and never pick it up again. Every instance of temptation presented me with a choice, and it was my responsibility to decide how I would respond. I had to see God as bigger than any stronghold and thank Him and believe it would be done according to His will and intention for my life.

What also became evident was the need to adjust the blame game and deal with the real origin of my anger. Anger in itself was not a sin; but unchecked, it was a sure path to destruction, and mine was misdirected at everything and everyone. We wrestle against the forces of darkness that the enemy subjects to our lives, but we have to come to the light of our accountability for the access we permitted through silence or behavior that supported his efforts. Increase in the knowledge of God helped me to see how wrong living made it difficult to stand in battle. What became apparent in my change therapy was that God, who was at work in my brokenness, had the power to turn it all around for good and use it for His purpose. I was well on my way to change where the fruit of life was sure to manifest in myself as well as the relationships with my parents and my children.

***

Change has nothing to do with how we begin but has everything to do with how we finish. Like infants, we didn't come into the world walking or running for that matter. We underwent a process; and there were trips, stumbles, and falls along the way. In our most dire times and trying situations, we must keep in mind that our steps have been ordered by the Lord, and He uses every experience to build in us a compelling testimony. We must first have a desire *(heart)* to change and our thoughts *(mind)* set on change, and I took the necessary steps.

***

CHAPTER TEN
WHAT WILL YOUR LEGACY BE?

Ephesians 2:10 *"For we are God's masterpiece. He has created us anew in Christ Jesus, so we can do the good things he planned for us long ago."* (NLT)

Along with change came a deeper understanding of the magnitude of my narrative and the impact it would have on those around me. This understanding also came with a perspective adjustment, and I really wanted to leave the world a little different than I found it, especially for the sake of my children. Self aside, I needed the generational curses to end with me, and my story needed to climax with what would prepare them for their lives and the journey ahead filled with mountains and valleys, twists and turns, and winding roads.

There was no how-to manual with play-by-play instructions for how to navigate through the pathways designed for them or how to overcome the obstacles placed in front of them. Besides, if what we endured were like lights switched in the on position, hope would shine forth in times of darkness for those who journeyed after us. If I *could* leave an instruction manual behind, I would instruct my children to avoid the mistakes I made. I would also teach them never to give up no matter how difficult life became, to remain mindful that everything has purpose, and to spy for wisdom gained from life's challenges.

People don't readily remember much of what we say to them, but they will remember how we made them feel. Actions speak much louder than words. What we did concerning a matter weighs more heavily than what we said about it. I started laying the foundation for my children as early as age ten for my son and age five for my daughter. Even while I struggled to get my life back on track, I told them to pursue their goals and dreams. I couldn't expect them to do so without them witnessing it first in me. From an education standpoint, my son and daughter attended my college graduation, saw me walk the stage and receive my degree. Subsequently, they both graduated high school and went on to experience college life.

I started thinking there had to be more. What else could I leave behind for my family – a name, maybe? Names play a significant role in our lives, and, at the very end, an obituary will be written and then read. This brief synopsis will include a date of birth, date of death, and the names of parents, siblings, children, grandchildren, nieces, nephews, and so forth. What the obituary doesn't state is what was left behind, how we contributed to the world around us, or if our family or community reaped anything from our lives.

Everything I went through was not for the sake of boasting that I made it but to pay it forward for others who may experience some of the same struggles and adversities. We all have gifts within us, often manifold in measure, and the collection of events along life's journey supports the construct of our message to be shared with a hurting world. Singing, writing, speaking, and playing instruments are a sample set of talents that provide the platform for our gifts to be shared with a broader audience. Our message should be a beacon of light that shares a message of hope with future overcomers – a legacy that carries on well after our time in the earth expires.

One of the ambitions of the enemy is to destroy the woman. Women are seed carriers – nurturers who birth kings and queens from their wombs. The unborn are the promise seeds of purpose for which she travails until the appointed time for them to manifest. The enemy fears the outcome of the womb, for, in God, the will of the seed would be another who would defeat the plan of the enemy in his/her life.

He who began a good work in us shall surely complete it.[7] We must be diligent to stay in His word and live out our faith in demonstration. Heaven's resources are made available and angels are encamped around us to ensure the timely delivery of His offspring – His heritage – additions to His legacy.

My living legacy would be to speak the truth to all who would hear, change mindsets, and reprogram thinking to transform every *"I can't"* to an *"I can."* Every thought is a seed, and the negative ones we meditate on about ourselves become thoughts of destruction. If we allow those thoughts to dictate our responses, we will also adversely impact the lives of our families, strengthen generational curses, and reinforce ungodly strongholds. Then we would be contributors to a community that is physically and spiritually weak and poor.

Equally dangerous is the love of living for the world and the things in it. This generation is very different from those in the recent past. We live like emergencies are non-existent and are rarely prepared for anything in advance. Now when the unforeseen happens, we rush to the aid of Go Fund Me accounts, online donations, and the like, when there should have been a safety net in place before the bottom fell out. God equips us to provide for our families and bless others around us. We should fall back on Him in our time of need and depend on Him to be our crisis-intervention specialist.

Attempts to be justified or vindicated in or by the world are fruitless. There is life beyond our current circumstances, and we don't have to abort what lies ahead or settle for now events. Many of us were chosen to be trailblazers – pioneers of sorts – and a part of a heavenly legacy. A large number of philanthropists and great leaders started from meager beginnings. What if we were handpicked to join the ranks of those called to spearhead the way for others? To whom much is given, much is required,[8] but so is the opportunity afforded to tap

---

[7] Philippians 1:6 paraphrased

[8] Luke 12:48 paraphrased

into the greatness God deposited. He is invested in His legacy of which we can be an integral part.

I believe when we stop hiding our testimonies and break the silence, more people will be healed. I would encourage others not to run from the past but use it to demonstrate its contribution to who they are becoming. God may intend for our lives to impact one or a hundred but what we've endured, even the most traumatic occasions and sometimes unjust in nature, were meant to work for His glory. The transformed life is the message of the gospel; the good news that, like Christ, we can live again and encourage those who come along after us, and that is a more-than-worthy legacy.

CHAPTER ELEVEN
NEW JOURNEY

Joshua 14:11 *"I am still as strong today as the day Moses sent me out; I'm just as vigorous to go out to battle now as I was then."* (NIV)

Despite hardships, I was always able to find safe refuge in the midst of hostile surroundings. I gained fortitude from those retreat havens and found the strength to press on. I stood when I wanted to faint and said, *"Yes, you can,"* when I wanted to quit. I never understood why I fought so hard when I was already knocked down, but something on the inside kept saying, *"Kimberly, get up!"* Hence, my new journey began with a made up mind to do exactly that.

Fearfully and wonderfully made is what the scriptures say about me. I was well beyond 426, the place where I knew comfort as a little girl, and was now unrecognizable because a transformation had taken place. The adversities and dark moments were the hiding places of development, and, as promised, God was rendering order out of what appeared as chaos. 426, the place where faith was taught was also the place where pain was introduced. Although there was no turning back, the memories remained; and every lesson from then until now arranged the scenarios that brought me to this point in my life.

I resumed my writing and poured out what was inside of me. The hurt little girl wasn't as weak and fragile as before. I was stronger and no longer blinded by the things of the world that once caused me to stumble. I perceived the lies, falsehoods, and betrayals; and outward appearances were no longer adequate to conceal the years of damage that had to be addressed. Substitutes, such as relationships, affairs, careers, or nice homes, were unsuitable to heal the wounds or fill the voids.

Writing became my medicine, and from it evolved great power and determination, and the words of life I penned reversed the declarations of death once spoken through my anguish. I recorded my life events and gained a clearer sense of direction. I needed to journal so I wouldn't forget what God had done thus far.

I was determined to remove any remaining facades that impaired my vision. To avoid being entirely rejected, I relaxed my standard then set my sights far beneath it. It was one thing to be humble but something very different and almost degrading to believe I didn't deserve more; and, as a result, my self-esteem was cloaked in passive-aggressive behavior. I wanted to be loved, but I never fully healed from the violations of rape and molestation and I could no longer replace the memory of unwanted touches with made-up incidents. I was working on forgiving others, but the wounds their actions left behind were more deeply rooted.

It was time to let go of the other gods in my life – alcohol, partying, and men who meant me no good – and turn back to God. Both He and my family wanted me back, but my family reminded me that I could go no further unless I was entirely devoted to my faith and that they too would suffer casualty and be affected if I defaulted. This new journey was nothing short of life or death. Nothing was going to prevent me from engaging in the battles necessary to win the war over my soul. Persistence prevailed on my behalf and gave me strength to stand. Even the voids began to have purpose, and the noise of discontentment was muffled. Then I clearly heard the voice of God directing me back to Him. He was saying, *"This is the way, Kimberly. Now walk in it."* [9]

One of my spiritual sisters said that we were all called and ordained for something. Oftentimes, the pain, suffering, and shame that came

---
[9] Isaiah 30:21 paraphased

to rob us of our light and life were directly associated with the *"what"* we were called and chosen to do. The aftermath of every storm left residue and rubble of ash and loss yet served as obscurity for the *"why"* we had to endure so much. They also provided shelter and protection for the gifts, ministry, and transparency of testimony born out of diverse trials.

Women seem to endure much by way of pain and brokenness and are often underappreciated. We have somehow become silenced and victimized by a society that still aims to objectify us. Even young girls today have accepted being treated like objects and don the uniform through what is called trend and fashion. We have a voice, and it's time to speak up. It's time to speak out; not just for us but also for the generations of sons and daughters who come from us.

Women are not objects or victims but nurturers of nations birthed from within us. As women, we should never be quieted by guilt or shame or subjected to defend ourselves against acts committed against us. With my voice, I choose to utter words of healing; and I forgive my violators, even the one who wouldn't take no for an answer. I ask for mercy on his behalf and inner conviction of his wrongdoing that might release him of any strongholds formed as a result. I desire the same for him that I seek to obtain for myself – FREEDOM. Truly, I recognize that I am not the woman I used to be but love and appreciate the woman I am becoming.

***

After being in New York for eight months, I moved into my own apartment. I sat on a bare floor, and there I continued to write until my parents furnished the place with what I needed. I poured myself into my writing because I needed to invest in what would not only produce tangible evidence of the new journey but also chronicle the stages of my life on my way to my best possible self. Aside from wanting to leave behind a legacy for my children, I wanted proof that I could not only pursue but accomplish goals and dreams, both small and large. Hence, *Finding Love and Healing in the Pen* was born.

Along the road of this new journey, I discovered things about myself I never knew existed and took on challenges I would have previously shied away from. I went from working as a teacher's assistant, leading Sunday school, and teaching lessons from the bible to writing my first novel and accepting public speaking engagements; all of which seemed impossible.

Leaders aren't necessarily those who are found out front. The best trained began in the background – in obscurity and were the first to go through in order to lead others. Take Harriet Tubman, for example. If she had not found the way out through the underground passage, how could she lead others to freedom? Good leaders raise up other leaders, and great leaders lead by example.

I grew to accept that God's plans were much bigger than even my own ability. He entrusted me with a huge mission I needed Him to accomplish, and it was my turn to pay it forward.

***

Was the journey easy? Was it supposed to be? The journey required learning to die to self daily and the risk of vulnerability during the humbling process while areas of pride were removed. I still had flaws and much to conquer. I also had a lot to learn, especially about faith and trust. Each segment presented new challenges, but I managed by taking small steps on my way to accomplishing a huge goal. Was there a destination? Most certainly, but only God knows the what, where, when, and how. There was much to overcome strategically designed for my defeat... but I was destined to WIN!

CHAPTER TWELVE
BEING VALIDATED

Psalm 139:14 *"Thank you for making me wonderfully complex! Your workmanship is marvelous-how well I know it."* (NLT)

One of my favorite biblical narratives is the woman at the well. Her name wasn't mentioned, but what we know from the story was that she was from Samaria, and while she went to the well to draw water to drink, she encountered a Man who knew her. He knew where she had been, all she had done, how long she'd done it, and with whom. He knew EVERYTHING about her.

He also introduced Himself as the living water that would satisfy her thirst fully. Like this woman, many of us put forth great effort to relieve the symptom of a problem and fail to actually resolve the problem. This woman visited the well and found need to return each time she was depleted of what brought only temporary relief to the dry and parched areas of her life. Oftentimes, quick fixes bring increased severity to our pre-existing condition and leave us more broken and dissatisfied. That too was my narrative until I was reminded one day of His promises never to leave or abandon me and to fill up the dry and empty places.

***

So, why was it so important for me to post recaps of the Sunday sermons and stories of God's love and forgiveness? They were eye-openers, and I was drawn to the characters and their struggles because they were similar to my own. God loved and blessed them, and I wanted to simulate real-time encounters and share His truth with others through the words and notations I penned. I wanted to capture the love notes He left behind at specific phases as His personal impressions upon our hearts to remind us that we are His children and we were created with a purpose. *No one else can do what we were designed to do. Our lives were written as a message to others – either as a warning or example.*

While I was diligent to share so much with others, I failed to acknowledge my own worth. I deserved to be loved and accepted, and it was time to stop being so judgmental and set aside the self-condemnation. When people offered to be there for me, I had to swallow my pride and allow them beyond the taped-off boundary. He was leading me down a wonderful path; one that taught me to believe the power and promises of God for myself. I stopped looking to be validated by others but found validation through dependence in God's unfailing love. Besides, He was there from the very beginning and was the only One who delivered me from the dark places of hopelessness and despair.

Yes, we were born with an innate desire to be accepted, approved of, and validated. We often seek it from parents, family, friends, relationships, marriage, and now even on social media, but there is only One who won't fail us. We were approved from the moment He ordained our first breath. The sooner we realize that God has already approved us in the seasons He pre-determined, the sooner we'll recognize the doors opened to us and discern the people divinely positioned on the other side of them.

It may not have been in God's will for me to face such atrocities, but He definitely intended for me to survive them. There was a time when I wanted to die, and, today, I am glad He didn't give into that demand. Instead, I too met a Man who sent a Man so that I would never have to thirst again nor have to rely on counterfeit sources of strength and validation.

He put His power in me – the power to change – and a determination to write my way through to finding healing and love again. He'll do the same for you.

Healing begins within;

Before the words are spoken;

Formed from a place of vulnerability;

A place of honesty and openness.

Deep within –

CHAPTER THIRTEEN
LED BY GOD, LEAD BY EXAMPLE

In the opening segments, I spoke about *unlikely sources* – vessels used by God to convey His message. They are people who are often overlooked and underestimated; who question what they could possibly contribute to God's plan for mankind. In the scriptures, there were many *unlikely sources* He raised up, equipped, and empowered to deliver messages of life, hope and fulfillment to others through their unusual encounters. Many of them became great examples of faith and continue to encourage us today.

Being Hannah

Imagine Hannah's predicament when everyone else around her seemed to prosper. They discovered what they were called to accomplish, and their talents and gifts supported that calling. What of they, who, instead of using what they were afforded to uplift and encourage others, flaunted about and taunted others with their good fortune? It just so happened that Hannah was such a one who was targeted for such cruelty. She was loved; endeared even by her husband, but it failed to fill the emptiness she encountered during a season of bareness.

In Hannah's story, there was one in particular, Peninnah, who with great intention vexed Hannah in such a way that inflicted great harm. She lived in a home where chaos and strife took up residence where peace was supposed to abide. Although Peninnah appeared to have it all, could it be that she was lacking and envied Hannah because she was loved? What if Peninnah was a lesson of what could happen when pride and oppressive behavior are the prominent displays in our character? I've heard it said that power can change you. Do we then use the blessings of God as weapons to oppress and lord over others? Was is not He who had power to bring forth life from what appeared barren?

Throughout life, even before the onset of trials and adversity, God equips others to assist those who are called to endure. Many fail to realize that those adverse situations or circumstances in the lives of others are opportunities to give comfort, aid, shelter, or share whatever God has provided in abundance, but many choose to withhold what they were given for that purpose. Oftentimes, the hidden motive embedded in their rejection is envy. Most likely, they are aware of the capacity for greatness in those going through a time of tragedy. If they were *truly* focused on what they were called to do, the need to compete or feel threatened by the potential of another would be eliminated from the equation. What is not so readily recognized is that God is testing what's in their hearts by watching what they do with what He put in their hands.

God's *unlikely source*, Hannah, was barren, but God used her condition to give birth to her potential. Reading about Hannah revealed how those around her played a crucial part in her process.

Hannah was married to a man named Elkanah, who also had a second wife named Peninnah, who was responsible for the chaos, cruelty, and strife in Hannah's life. The pain Hannah suffered from not being able to bear children was intensified by the way she was treated by Peninnah, who had many children. Her taunting amplified the situation and highlighted the desire for what Hannah constantly yearned for. She had an advantage over Hannah because she contributed to her husband's legacy by having children. Although Peninnah caused problems in the household, the hidden root was that Hannah was favored of God and preferred by their husband. No matter how Elkanah showered Hannah with his love and many gifts, nothing compared to what God planned to do through her.

Hannah did not retaliate against Peninnah for her harsh treatment and abrasive behavior. Like Hannah, we can't afford to be offended by how others treat us. Oftentimes, they are wrestling with their own insecurities exposed by the light in us. Over time, Hannah overcame Peninnah because she relied on God's strength and did not give power to her weaknesses; and the more her rival taunted, the more she leaned on God. Hannah emptied herself out before the Lord, and He intervened on her behalf. When we examine Hannah's character, she maintained her piety and was free from guilt and wickedness even in her suffering.

God heard Hannah's cry and received her vow, and she gave birth to a son, Samuel, and dedicated the gift of her womb back to God for His set apart purposes. Beyond the womb, she continued to nurture her child and raised him up in the things of God. Samuel was the great seed of potential on the inside of Hannah. Undoubtedly, the process was rough, but the wait was well worth the outcome. This birth was not about Hannah but about God. Hannah's womb was the assigned place for the nurturing, nourishing, and development of the seed until it was time to come forth. Hannah displayed wisdom and was an example of the appropriate conduct during times of adversity. Circumstances, at best, are only temporary, but God will use them to prepare for what will sustain.

My Peninnah experience was not something I was very proud of. I knew what I wanted, but I was not mature enough to handle it at the time. I still needed to grow up and catch up to the me that waited up ahead. I saw people doing what I had a passion for with ease and watched some lording over others, while all I wanted was a chance to display goodness and give back. As I looked on, jealousy and pride emerged, but I had to learn to wait on God. There were already enough people doing more harm than good, and if I launched ahead too soon, I probably would have been numbered along with them.

I took my problem areas before the Father in prayer so that I could engage His reconstruction process. I felt barren and empty, but my heart had to change. Compassion was not something I could pick and choose who to extend to. I struggled with my motives – why I wanted those things and who I wanted them for. Was it for His glory, or did I have a hidden agenda? I had to be willing to dedicate back to God whatever He blessed me with and use how He chose to manifest Himself in my life for His glory.

I wanted to become a world-renowned motivational speaker. I thought about the money, buying a home, and obtaining financial freedom. Now, there was nothing wrong with that, but I neglected to make any mention of using that platform to tell others that God loves them and that they matter to Him. One of my mentors told me to remain in the vein from which I started when God opened doors for me. At first, I didn't understand why she told me that, but she knew of my not-so-good tendencies and wanted me to be aware of myself.

What I learned from this story was that challenges are a part of the process, and if Hannah had been distracted and lost faith, she would have missed her spiritual transformation. Instead, she allowed the adversity to discipline her, and she ultimately reaped the reward of the peaceable fruit of righteousness. Dealing with Peninnah was not a light matter, but success and breakthrough were included in the perfect timing of God. Don't despise Peninnah; she was vital to the story – a chosen instrument of refinement to prove Hannah on her way to overcoming.

Through God, we have the power to endure injustice and unpleasant situations. When the seed of the word of God is cultivated within, our outwardly conduct will be exemplary and evidence of our bearing fruit of the Spirit. Prayer is key, and we must ask of the Lord concerning His will for our lives. Then He, at the assigned time, will release what is needed to accomplish His will through us. The process is imperative, or we'll get ahead of or fall behind divine timing and strategy. Challenging circumstances reveal who we are and what's in us as well as what we need to improve. We cannot allow the opinions, influences, or expectations of others to cause us to abort the process lest pride take root and separate us from latter outcomes.

Some experiences may be Peninnah-like in nature. The pressure may even be unbearable at times, but it produces the anointing to equip us for His purpose – to reveal the best the world has yet to encounter. The strength to do all God has asked resides in the One who called us to it. Of course, it's painful to watch others enjoy what we hope to have or even long for, especially when we're going through because we've been obedient to all He has asked of us. What God intends to manifest through us has the propensity to make an indelible imprint in the lives of those we are called to impact.

CHAPTER FOURTEEN
WHO WILL YOU BE LOYAL TO?

Being Joseph

Many have heard the story of Joseph, who was a gifted young man and loved by his father. His brothers, however, despised him; and one would be tempted to speculate that Joseph's eagerness to share his dream was the cause of their dissention.

Joseph was shown a vision for a later time of his life, and he knew God planned to do something great through him. It was more likely that Joseph was excited to share what he saw with his brothers, but, instead, they perceived him as a braggart. Imagine being Joseph with preempted foresight of a position of elevation over the ones who mistreated and overlooked you? Despite his brothers' evil plan to kill him, that was exactly what happened.

Joseph was extremely gifted, but I'm sure he was not aware of how much adversity he would endure before he reached his ultimate potential. He endured injustice of every kind, yet he remained faithful; he remained loyal, and those around him saw that God was with him. Not everyone was upset over Joseph's anointing, and many benefitted from the gift deposited on the inside of him even during his times of hardship and difficulty. In what seemed like his darkest moments, people worked to his advantage and furthered God's purpose through Joseph.

Joseph had a gift of interpreting dreams but displayed humility and gave honor to the giver of his gifting when asked to interpret and give understanding. He often responded, *"I cannot do it, but God will."* [10]Joseph did not boast of his own ability, nor did he flaunt about as if it was something he manifested on his own. He chose not the path of immorality, nor did he assist others in plans of wrongdoing, not even for the approval of his peers. He never mocked, ridiculed, or put others down; and he always chose the way that honored his Father by doing only what was asked of him. This enabled him to prosper and those around him to be blessed.

We can't possibly understand the plans God has arranged for our lives. If He revealed all we had to go through, many of us would lack the courage to take the first step. God revealed the destiny to Joseph, and there were things omitted purposely, like being thrown into a pit and then sold into slavery by his brothers. He was also falsely accused of sexual impropriety and misconduct by Potiphar's wife and thrown into prison. Joseph's faith was tested rigorously.

Let's face it, it doesn't require as much to prepare for an exam if we already know what's on the test. Knowledge of the entire picture would omit the need to endure because prior knowledge would reveal exactly when and how it would end as well as what to avoid. Who would really willingly go through such hardship and injustice without wanting to run the other way? As human beings, we work from the beginning to the end, but God works from the end to the beginning, and nothing that happens catches Him by surprise. Our steps have been ordered – where we've been, where we are right now, and where we're going. He holds the reason and determines how long the season.

Finding our place and purpose can be very exciting and, at the same time, pose great challenge to refrain from running off and doing our own thing, especially when faced with life's difficulties and fear of risk-taking. The walk of faith isn't an easy one, but believing our way is better than God's way is a dangerous course of action. Disobedience will move us out from the will of God, and defiance will only lead to a life of constant and unnecessary struggles. Discovering

---
[10] Genesis 41:16 NIV

purpose and destiny does not mean we've arrived; it only means that we've been selected to endure the refinement process. We can take notes from Joseph's life and be careful not to share everything with everyone. Sometimes, the very person(s) we confide in may be envious of what God wants to do in our lives. Surprisingly, there are people who are positioned to discourage, disturb, distract, and disrupt the process and qualify as the instruments of refinement secured to assist in our process.

I appreciate those who God placed in my life; those who didn't give up or turn away, who stayed true to the course and remained faithful. Because of the lessons they learned, they, in turn, reach, teach, and share their wisdom and guidance. God raised up leaders in the bible to restore the life back to those who experienced famine-like circumstances. He will use our lives to testify to others as well. When God takes us through, we often become unrecognizable to some and just what was expected to others He revealed us to. Joseph's story teaches us a valuable lesson on how to avoid hatred and bitterness. When he was established in the place God ordained, despite disloyalty from his family members, his heart was moved to compassion; and he did well by those who had done him wrong – a display of great strength and godly character.

Obedience to God mandates us to forgive, not only those we love or who love us but is also extended to our enemies – those who wronged us. Remember, all things work for the good of those that love God and are the called according to His purpose.[11] We may face a few obstacles in our lives that appear to block our miracle, but God can either remove those obstacles, give us wisdom and direction to go around them, or fortify us to go through them. Joseph's dream came with huge sacrifices. If God showed him everything pertaining to the abundance he would receive, his motives may have been compromised as well as his devotion to God, and he would have forgone the great lessons taught by faith.

---

[11] Romans 8:28 paraphrased

Can God Really Trust Us With The Vision?

Will we remain committed to God in the face of adversity, when the hardships are vital to our process and navigate us to the finish line? There's a lesson embedded in every phase that qualifies us to move to the next level. I never expected so many different distractions along the way. Why was I going through so many hassles? Initially, I envisioned something glitzier and thought more about my desires and rewards instead of what my gift was intended for.

I wanted to start another project, but my inner voice warned and said, *"No, not yet."* This assignment had everything to do with how He intended to use my love for writing for my own personal healing and to ignite the healing process in others. When God begins to move, we should fasten our seat belts and affix our eyes straight ahead because if we look to the left or the right, we may be tempted to pull aside and the blessing intended for us may pass us by.

Have faith and stay focused because; and despite it all, we are favored by God. Stay in His will, and He will give us the desires of His heart.

***

www.ingramcontent.com/pod-product-compliance
Lightning Source LLC
Chambersburg PA
CBHW072010290426
44109CB00018B/2197